Dare to hope

90 day devotional

By Amy Lennox

Copyright © 2022

Dedicated to my mum, Marjorie Bennett.
Always believed I would write this but never got to
see it.

Acknowledgements

To all who sent many messages of encouragement to write this book.

Thank you to my good friend, Alison Kernohan, who offered to proofread this devotional for me. I know she put so much effort into ensuring this was the best it could be!

Also to my husband, Jonny Lennox, who formatted the book, designed the cover, and always encouraged me in writing this!

"I thank my God in all my remembrance of you"
Phil 1:3

Day 1
Dare to Hope
"FOR BY GRACE YOU HAVE BEEN SAVED...."
EPHESIANS 2:8

I called this devotional book, 'Dare to Hope' to try and encourage those of you reading to hope. Hope is a word used by people in many different circumstances, for example, I hope they get into that school, and I hope they get the right results. Hope can be an overused word in today's culture and has often lost the meaning that it first had in the original language in which the Bible was written. Looking at the original language, 'hope' actually has multiple meanings. The primary meaning overall is having confidence and expectation.

In many situations it is difficult to hope. That is why I am calling this book 'Dare to Hope.' As Christians, we have a confident hope that we cannot lose through any pandemic or difficulty we face. If you belong to Jesus you have the sure hope that your sins are forgiven and you have received the gift of eternal life. We also have a secure hope that is steadfast through any storm we may meet, our hope lies in Jesus Christ. Our hope has never been in ourselves; our true hope has never been or should never have been in what we have or what we can do. Our hope should always lie in Jesus Christ. He is steadfast, faithful, never changing and always there, and because of that, we have a never-ending hope.

Maybe you do not know Jesus yet and have no faith. I encourage you to take time out of each day to search for the hope that we have, and to read this book with an open heart and mind. Engage with the Bible as you read each day. The Word of God is far more important than my own words; they are what will transform your life!

Maybe you have been finding it hard to hope recently. I encourage you to take a ninety day challenge and read through

3

this book. I pray that while you do, you will dare to hope again and look to Jesus for all that you need. He is the one we can always depend on no matter what we face. We can never reach the end of our expectations of Jesus.

Maybe you are firm in your faith, may I challenge you to take ninety days and dare to hope more? Maybe you have got comfortable in your faith. Let's start to search for more profound knowledge of what we already know of God.

I challenge you to dare to hope. Are you ready?

Day 2
Dare to hope again

"GOD IS OUR REFUGE AND STRENGTH, A VERY PRESENT HELP IN TROUBLE."
PSALM 46:1

I could still take you down the hospital corridor that I walked every day for those ten days. Mum was lying in room 19 on the 4th floor. She had been diagnosed with cancer in June 2020, and it was now September 2020. Cancer had taken over faster than any of us had been prepared for. We went in every day those ten days waiting for the final goodbye to come here on earth.

I had a four-month-old at home along with my two-year-old daughter. It wasn't what any of us had planned. It wasn't a journey I had wanted in any way to walk, especially at that time. If you have had any children, you will know how much you depend on your mum in those early days. She had just started teaching me how to mother multiple children when she got her diagnosis. She had worked for God her whole life, and she had just retired. She had dreams and plans that were now all cut down as she lay up in the hospital bed.

How do you hope in times like that? My mum taught me how. Every morning when we were younger, she would have her Bible in front of her. I remember every night before bed how we prayed together. I remember her teaching us, praying with us, explaining to us and feeding herself with the truth of God's promises. She didn't wait until she needed to know these things for herself. She didn't wait until she needed to experience God as a refuge and strength to start reading the Bible. She laid the foundation every day when times were good, so that when times were hard, she had a strong stance for the battle that lay ahead.

She never questioned if God was good, she knew He was. She never asked if God's plan was right, she knew it was. She never

5

doubted because she knew her God well before the storm hit, and so she dared to hope when times were hard.

I want to encourage you today, if times are good for you at the moment, to build your foundation, to know that God is your refuge and strength before the storms hit. Pray, read, search, question, worship, set aside time for you and God to build that relationship in your everyday life before anything rocks your world, so when you are hit, you are strong in the storm in your refuge and strength.

How do you hope if you are facing hard times? How do you dare to hope again?

Get a relationship with Jesus sorted in your life. Remember all the times He has helped you in the past and write them down. Ask other people to pray for you because the power of prayer can change things. Ask for help from people you trust, and most of all, go to God who is your refuge and strength and be honest with Him. He can and will be your strength in times of trouble. He will walk beside you all the way if you come to Him, you aren't on your own.

Dare to hope again, your story does not have to end here.

Day 3
Dare to believe

"FOR ALL THE PROMISES OF GOD FIND THEIR YES IN HIM. THAT IS WHY IT IS THROUGH HIM THAT WE UTTER OUR AMEN TO GOD FOR HIS GLORY."
2 CORINTHIANS 1:20

I experienced a miscarriage with our first baby back in July 2017. It began in June 2017. As I was doing my devotionals, I was reading 2 Kings 4:16-17 "About this season, about this time next year you shall embrace a (child)...and she bore a (child) about that time, the following spring." We hadn't planned to have children at this point, so this came as a bit of a shock. However, I kept it to myself and told God that His plan was always best. The following month I found out I was pregnant and was due in the spring. Obviously, I accepted this was the promise and told Jonny the whole story, and we waited, and then two weeks later, we lost the baby.

Of course, I mourned the loss of our baby; however, the miscarriage also left us confused! Did we read the Bible wrong? Did I hear God wrong? Was it not actually meant for us? Questions ran through our heads. However, a song, 'Yes and Amen' played in the car on the way home from the hospital. Even though our situation seemed lost, we made a conscious decision, and we were going to keep believing in God even when it seemed like the promise was gone! Even though we were in the darkness and couldn't see the light, we chose to believe.

I remember standing in the office one day praying about all that had happened and looking out the window. I was struggling to believe what God had said and at that moment a full arch rainbow appeared before me right in front of our house as I stood there. A rainbow was a sign God gave to Noah which symbolises that He always keeps His promises. So I grabbed my phone and took a photo, which I had saved on my phone ever since to help me keep choosing to believe even when it was a struggle. A month later, I was pregnant, and we had a baby born in the spring—fulfilment of the promise.

Maybe, today, you have received a promise from God a long time ago and are still waiting on the fulfilment of that promise. Maybe you have only just received a promise but circumstances around you are making it difficult for you to keep believing. It can be hard, especially when circumstances make you feel like the promise is literally dying within you and you do not have any other place to turn to.

Let me encourage you, God is faithful and He will keep His promise. It may not be in the way we hoped for, or would like it to be, but God always keeps His promises. If you have a promise and feel like giving in to the feeling that it will never happen, keep believing. God will bring it to pass in His timing, as He is never in a rush. We must choose to trust and believe. It is a conscious decision that only you can make.

It will make all the difference in your life if you dare to believe and keep believing, what God has promised you.

Day 4
Dare to remember
**"BUT THIS I CALL TO MIND, AND THEREFORE I HAVE HOPE."
LAMENTATIONS 3:21**

Hannah told me one day, "I used to need to fed when I was a little girl."

She "remembers" things from when she was little based on what Emily does. She has been using this phrase a lot lately. But "remembering" these things helps her realise how far she has come and how much of a "big girl" she has become.

Sometimes we have to remember. As I shared in the devotional on day 2, mum died in September 2020 and I have been remembering her a lot. Remembering can be painful, but it can also be so helpful in reminding us how far we have come from where we were.

Lamentations is a book of Jeremiah pleading to God for help from a critical state. Chapter 3 speaks about how he has "forgotten happiness and... his endurance has perished.". There was a day through the first Covid-19 lockdown I think I hit the lockdown wall: constant childcare, constant lock-in, constant rain. I hit a wall where I felt like my endurance had perished from everything I had faced the last year. How many of us feel like this?

Maybe you feel the same, but the writer goes on to say, "But this I call to mind, and therefore I have hope." He remembers the Lord's faithfulness, the Lord's love and the Lord's mercy. His spirit lifts, and He has renewed hope.

Hope is sometimes hard to find in life's ups and downs. Many have lost loved ones, business, friends and family. What do you need to remember to find that hope again?

Maybe you need to look back and see God's faithfulness in your life. Perhaps you need to remember God's love for you and your family.

Could it be that if you remembered God's provision and protection, you would be able to hope again? It can be easy to forget all of God's goodness to us when things are going against us, especially if there is a consistent barrage of issues, problems or conflict that we are facing. It can be difficult when friendship breaks down or when money is tight or when family issues keep reappearing to remember that God is still good, still sees you and still cares about you.

Sometimes in life we have to physically tell ourselves to remember. We have to have good chat with our mind, will and emotions to make them remember that God is good, kind, faithful and constant. We have to remember all God has done for us in the past to help us face the future. Call them to mind, ponder on them write them down, look up your old promises from Heaven and remember. God is still the SAME God, and He never changes and never leaves you. But sometimes we have to force ourselves and choose.

You have to remember, dare to remember, and hope will follow.

Day 5
Dare to tremble
"THE LORD REIGNS; LET THE PEOPLE TREMBLE."
PSALM 99:1

Jonny and I always take a wee half-day away from everything to think for the first week of the New Year. It provides an opportunity to ponder and think about the year ahead.

Last year on my day, as I drove to get coffee and find somewhere to sit and read and think, I was listening to the news. It was overwhelming, lockdown again, exams cancelled again, lives uncertain and the futures of many once more looked dim.

I drove up, parked, opened my coffee and opened my Bible to Psalm 99:1 "The Lord reigns, let the people tremble." the first words I read.

What a complete comfort in times of uncertainty to read that the Lord reigns. He still reigns. Even in the middle of a pandemic, He reigns and He isn't panicked. He knows what He is doing, and He knows the plan, and His goal for you is still for good and not evil even though circumstances may point differently. It is the Lord who reigns. Not an angel, not any other created being who is imperfect and can make decisions based on emotions or opinions. The Lord never changes, or acts rashly, or for His own good. He always is the same forever and ever and so we can trust Him.

I then wondered, why do the people tremble?

Indeed if the Lord reigns, it should say, "let the people live in joy and peace?" I would assume because the Lord reigns we should be happy and content and excited because no matter what happens, God is in control. Why does David use the word tremble?

I believe it is because while the Lord reigns, it means we have to relinquish control to Him. After all, we don't understand when or what or how He is working. I'm sure Noah didn't like being cooped up in an ark for over a year, or Jonah enjoyed sitting in a big fish, David didn't relish the prospect of facing a giant, or Mary becoming an outcast in society. However, all these occurred because the Lord reigned, and His plans were accomplished.

We know the end of their stories. We know how it all worked out, but when they were in the middle, I'm sure they trembled. We are still in the middle of God's reign, and we don't know what we will face along the path. I know some of us are trembling. Being angry and scared and anxious and fearful is OK, but we need to bring those emotions to God.

So, while we may tremble, we can rest assured that God holds us in the palm of His hand and under the safety of His wings, and we do not go through life alone because the Lord reigns.

May we be a people who dare to tremble because God reigns and we follow Him.

Day 6
Dare to trust

"TRUST IN THE LORD WITH ALL YOUR HEART, AND DO NOT LEAN ON YOUR OWN UNDERSTANDING. IN ALL YOUR WAYS, ACKNOWLEDGE HIM, AND HE WILL MAKE STRAIGHT YOUR PATHS." PROVERBS 3:5-6

I often think about Mary, the mother of Jesus throughout the year, especially since becoming a mummy. I'm not sure what time of the year you are reading this, but join me for a moment, will you?

Imagine a heavily pregnant girl on the back of a donkey. She and Joseph have travelled all day, every day, for possibly a month! Imagine the smell, the stress, the sweat, the unsterile environment they have encountered for days on end. They eventually make it to Bethlehem, and Mary's time draws close. The hard part is behind them, surely?

God knew they had to come here. Undoubtedly He has prepared a bed for them to lay on, a comfortable private room for them to have their firstborn! Imagine the frustration as they knocked door after door asking for help. The panic that set in when the innkeeper showed them to a stable. The helplessness they felt when they held a newborn baby, the most precious newborn baby, among the animal dung and the half-chewed hay.

Not the pretty nativity scene we often picture. The confusion they must have felt. Where is God in this? Why didn't He provide for us?

And yet God did and had planned this all for His big picture to take place. A newborn lamb was placed in a manger to signify that they were to be sacrificed in the future. A baby in a stable was a sign for all men that He had come for them. A baby born in Bethlehem was a sign that He was the promised king from prophecy spoke years ago. A baby born of a virgin was a

13

symbol of the miraculous and the purity of the baby as the baby's blood comes from the Father's line.

Amidst the panic and confusion and fear Mary probably felt, God's plan was coming together beautifully. At times in your life, I am sure confusion, panic, and fear have come strong. How amazing is it to think and believe that God's plan for you might just be coming together beautifully, and you don't even realise it?

I am so thankful that God's beauty can be seen even in the middle of what seems dirty and utterly impossible. In the middle of panic and what seems like complete absurdity, God still reigns. Even in the middle of being asked to do something that makes no sense to us, God still speaks.

As a mummy, I am so thankful I can leave my children at the feet of Jesus because His plan exceeds mine even in the midst of parenting chaos. As a person, I can trust God with my life because His plan is reigning despite the turmoil. As a Christian, I can believe that even when all around seems hopeless, I can accept God's plan is still coming together. Mary, did you know? Probably not.

If you're reading this, you don't know the end of your story either. Keep going, God is doing something in your life beyond what you can imagine. And we don't even realise.

Dare to hope and trust that God's plan continues to come together, even if it seems like a mess. His ways and His thoughts are higher than ours, He can see the bigger picture of where we are going and so we can trust in Him.

Day 7
Dare to be guided

"AND THE LORD WILL GUIDE YOU CONTINUALLY AND SATISFY YOUR DESIRE IN SCORCHED PLACES AND MAKE YOUR BONES STRONG AND YOU SHALL BE LIKE A WATERED GARDEN, LIKE A SPRING OF WATER, WHOSE WATERS DO NOT FAIL."
ISAIAH 58: 11

It snowed today, it was the first snow of the year and the first snow when our youngest and most adventurous child was a toddler. She was desperate to get out in the snow, so much that she found her wellies and coat and stood in the hall at the front door banging it until we would let her out. Eventually, we were ready, and we all went out into the snow. We live right beside the main road in our village, which isn't majorly busy but busy enough that you wouldn't want your toddler wandering out onto it by mistake. So I took on the role of the girls' guide while they played. I yelled stop if they went too far away and held hands in the tricky parts of the yard; I was there to help them up when they fell and helped them not fall face-first as they splashed through the puddles.

Why did I do that? Was it spoiling their fun and making them feel restricted and bound by rules instead of wanting to play and enjoy the snow? No! I guided them to keep them safe; I guided them because I could see further. I advised them because I was wiser and could see the path and any trouble ahead. I showed them because I loved them too much to leave them to play alone, vulnerable to danger.

Isaiah states in today's verse that God will guide us continually. Continually - that means every day you have a hard time, every moment you feel like you're about to lose the plot, every time you have a wrong thought, every day you can't express in words the grief you feel. Every celebration you have, every decision you have to make, every prayer you pray in desperation, every depressive episode you experience-God guides you through it all.

15

God guides you not because He wants to rule over you but because He loves you too much to leave you to try and find the way on your own. God guides you not because He dominates us but because He can see dangers ahead that we can't. God instructs us not because He is stopping our fun but because He wants to enrich our lives and allow us to live our lives in the best possible way.

God guides us continually, never-ending, never stopping, never slowing, never too fast, always at the right moment. He is a God who knows the right path for you and will never let you down as you seek it. How do we find His guidance? Through reading our Bible so we can hear Him, and praying through everything we face so we can speak to Him. God can show us the path ahead if we take time to listen and speak to Him about what we are facing.

Dare to hope in His guidance as you journey through the ups and downs of life.

Day 8
Dare to listen

"AND THE LORD WILL GUIDE YOU CONTINUALLY AND SATISFY YOUR DESIRE IN SCORCHED PLACES AND MAKE YOUR BONES STRONG. YOU SHALL BE LIKE A WATERED GARDEN, LIKE A SPRING OF WATER, WHOSE WATERS DO NOT FAIL."
ISAIAH 58: 11

In this passage in Isaiah, God has given the Jews a good talking to. As a parent, I sometimes have to sit our children down and explain to them what I mean when I am cross and what the right way to live is. It is not to make them feel small and worthless, but to build them up and help them live in the right way.

God was doing this for the Jews. He had seen that their motives were wrong, and that they were going about doing their own thing. God wanted them to know that He had a plan for their lives and what was acceptable to live for Him. He wanted them to cease oppressing others and instead help the needy and poor (Isaiah 58v6-7), and then He would answer their prayers.

Not only that, but He would also satisfy their desires and make their very core strong again. I don't know if you have ever tried to live a life that goes against what God intends for you. It doesn't lead to good things. You end up fighting a fight that you were never meant to fight. You lose your peace, you lose your support system, you lose everything that once made you content in God when you go against what He knows is best for us. Not because He wants to punish us but because He knows it will get our attention back to Him.

The Jews were in a hard place when God was speaking to them. They were feeling weak and depressed, and overwhelmed by all they were currently facing. They didn't understand what had gone wrong for them until they listened to God, and once they heard and followed what God commanded them to do for their good, God restored strength and blessings to them once again.

Maybe you are feeling weak and depressed, perhaps the love you once felt for God is missing, maybe it has been a while since you last read and prayed and listened to what God wanted for your life. You may feel like you are currently in a scorching place, feeling nothing but failure and pressure and oppression.

Maybe it is time for you to turn back to God, whom you once served fully, and listen to what He has to say. Not because He wants to rule or dominate you, but because He knows what is best for your life and wants to give you abundant life that only He can give. Dare to listen to Him again and see if there is something in your life you have missed and need to revive, maybe need to kill off, maybe need to set down, or some action you need to take to get right with God again. The start of today's verse says God will guide you continually. That doesn't just mean through the good or hard times, but also through the dry wilderness times you don't understand. He promises to guide you and help you see what you're missing.

Dare to hope that God has a plan for you, but maybe you have to make the first move and return to Him again. Dare to listen to what He said. It may just make a world of difference to you! He will make your very core strong, and God will quench your scorched, parched, dry feeling with water that will never run dry.

Day 9
Dare to be forgiven

"I HAVE BLOTTED OUT YOUR TRANSGRESSIONS LIKE A CLOUD AND YOUR SINS LIKE MIST; RETURN TO ME, FOR I HAVE REDEEMED YOU."
ISAIAH 44:22

We have two small girls and two dogs in our home. Our living room used to have a grey carpet in it, and believe me when I tell you, that carpet saw some abuse over eighteen months after we moved in. From potty training a toddler to potty training a puppy, vomit and poop explosions from both dogs and children. The carpet was worse for wear.

I tried all the carpet cleaners, I tried washing it down, I tried putting mats over the stains. Until the day finally came for us to rip it up, we could lay a new floor. When we ripped up the carpet, I was fit to see all the cleaning I had done was only superficial. There lay all the old stains just underneath the first layer. The stain our daughter made when she wasn't well. The stain our pup made when she was being trained. I could tell you what the stains were, and all my cleaning had just rid them from the surface. They were just underneath what others could see. The smell of them was there, and as soon as we touched the carpet, they were there.

It took ripping it up entirely to thoroughly clean the room from every stain.

How amazing is our God that when we come to Him, He doesn't merely pat us clean? He doesn't just use a fancy cleaner and hopes the stain goes away. Some of us have tried to "clean" ourselves only for the stain to remain just under the surface. As soon as we hit a bump or someone annoys us. The stench is apparent for all to see. You can maybe trace every stain in your life, where it came from and don't know how to get rid of it completely. You just hide it from the surface. We can try every good work, every good idea, every good church, but nothing is

19

ever enough to completely rid us of every stain we have picked up throughout our lives.

Isn't it amazing that God's grace alone is enough to entirely, totally and utterly rid your life from every stain for good. Not just semi-clean, completely clean.

Have you found His grace in your life yet? If not, ask Him for it today and stop trying to do it yourself. He is ready and willing to impart His grace to you so that you can get right with God and have a clean life.

If you have, give thanks because our God is so gracious to us, to show us mercy that we do not deserve by granting us grace that was fully paid for by His Son.

You can have a spotless life today. Not hidden, not leading a double life, nothing just below the surface you hope no one sees. A spotless, fresh life that you can use for His kingdom. That's the Good News of the Gospel. That's the glad tidings.

Dare to hope in forgiveness available to you. Hope in a God who can clean us from every stain- nothing too hard, nothing too small, nothing too disgraceful. God can do it for you. You simply need to ask!

Day 10
Dare to Lean
"I AM WHO I AM."
EXODUS 3:14

Who is your support system? It was once said, 'No man is an island." Isn't that a well known saying. We had to live like islands through the coronavirus lockdown. We were forced into isolation and loneliness, forced to rely on ourselves for help and support. So many of us lost the support systems that we once had. We all need one. The days we are living in are getting darker every day. More laws are being passed, more damage is being done, more confusion is being caused, and we each need a support system. We cannot face these things all by ourselves.

I remember asking God during one lockdown where I was feeling particularly nervous and shaken and panicked about who I should turn to for help. His reply was brief, but so good!
"I AM"

He gave the same reply to Moses out looking after sheep in the desert. God asked Him to abandon all and rescue His people. Moses inquired as to how he, a mere man, was going to rescue millions of people out of the grips of an evil king. God's response to Moses, "I AM."
And He responds to all of your questions today with the same reply- 'I AM'.

I am enough for you in these circumstances that you face.
I am your healer from every disease you face.
I am wisdom to help you know how to cope with difficult decisions.
I am protection over you and your household
I am comfort in isolation
I am provision in the middle of financial issues
I am the truth that overshadows lies

I am the life that conquers death
I am hope in despair
I am safety in fear
I am the light in the darkness
I am your guide in the division
I AM all you need.

He is who He has always been, and He will stay who He has always been. We may feel lost and alone, but He is not. He is the support system you can trust above anyone or anything else in your world.

You may have a social bubble; that's great. But they can't give you all you need. You may have a family; that's awesome. But they can't give you all you need. He is all you need and more. Why not declare some of these over your life, over your questions today that you are facing and don't know how you're going to make it through. Declare who God is over your situation today. Sometimes you just need to speak it out loud for the devil to hear and you to believe it!

Dare to lean on God, ask Him to be beside you and help you see that He really is who He says He is. And see the changes He can bring in your life.

Day 11
Dare to love
"A NEW COMMANDMENT I GIVE YOU, THAT YOU LOVE ONE ANOTHER."
JOHN 13:34

So many opinions have arisen over the past few years among many people. So many ideas and voices have risen in objection and support through much debate. The Church is getting caught up in arguments causing division that are based on secondary purposes to God's plans here on earth.

We want to make sure that we agree on fundamental beliefs, such as the Gospel, Jesus' birth, death and resurrection and return. However, secondary ideas can cause such division among people.

It's so easy to get caught up in ensuring that your opinion is heard above everyone else's. We can become so passionate about our stance that it overtakes everything else we see. Often our judgement can become clouded because someone disagrees with what you're doing.

The goal in the world's eye is to make sure your voice is heard, your opinion is raised, and you are put first. But is that our goal if we are Christ-followers? The devil thrives in division, in chaos, in confusion and arguments. He loves it when the Church is against themselves.

What is our goal if we are Christ-followers?
The goal is LOVE.

Love is our goal as the Church of Jesus, especially in times of division and debate. Love and respect each other. No matter what our opinion is, if we disagree, if you think I'm wrong- Love and respect each other. Paul said that the greatest of faith, hope and love is love, (1 Corinthians 13:13).

So when the world is all about shouting the loudest, when fear is prominent, and rejection is imminent, at a time when it's so easy to debate and argue with each other, let us be a Church that makes love the main goal in this world. Let love be a shining beacon that cuts through the chaos we face. "By this all people will know that you are my disciples, if you have love for one another" (John 13:35).

Dare to love and see what a difference it makes in your world when you look above other people's faults and begin to see them with love.

Day 12
Dare to praise

**"I WILL BLESS THE LORD AT ALL TIMES...I SOUGHT THE LORD, AND HE ANSWERED ME AND DELIVERED ME FROM ALL MY FEARS."
PSALM 34:1A, 4**

Jonny believes that Christmas is meant for December and not before. He even packs my Christmas socks away in the Christmas decorations box so I can't get them until we bring them down in December. However, this past year, I got a small real tree in November, put Christmas lights around it, and placed it on our doorstep. It twinkled and shone and brightened up the darkest of nights. Lights can make a difference in our world and our circumstances.

The world can feel intense and vulnerable, and dark at times. While it may sometimes feel like the news is dark, hope is dim, and everything we are facing is unclear- there is light in the darkness. Jesus described Himself as 'the Light of the World', John 8:12. Isn't it incredible that Jesus is not just a light, not a dim bulb glowing somewhere that can only show a small pathway before you. He is the Light—the Light for the World.

And this light enables us to pray to Him about everything we face and whatever happens. He frees us from all our fears. All our fears about the future, about family, about health: He frees us from all our worries! Maybe today you are sitting alone and vulnerable, and the pathway ahead in your world looks completely dark. You don't know what to do, where to turn, or who to call for help.

Jesus, the Light of the World, can help you be free from your fears if you ask Him to.

I wonder whether David wrote the line which declared the Lord would free him from fear before or after He decided to praise the Lord at all times!

Sometimes before we even experience the freedom God promises us, we need to start to praise Him. Praise where you are right now, even if circumstances don't change, even if laws and regulations tighten, even if news headlines become scary and the world looks dark, even if family matters don't pan Him out. Even if. I will praise the Lord at all times, and He will free me from all my fears!

The tree on my doorstep will sparkle and light the darkness, but for a season. The Lord is the Lord forever and never changes. That is the Light that sparkles in our darkness today and will never go out!

Dare to praise God even in the darkest of circumstances and you will see how it helps the situation look different even if nothing else has changed.

Day 13
Dare to Wait
"WAIT FOR THE LORD; BE STRONG AND LET YOUR HEART TAKE COURAGE. WAIT FOR THE LORD."
PSALM 27:14

I heard a story. It's one of those stories that you know will stay in your mind for a long time because it hit a cord. I wanted to share it with you.

It's about a man called David Livingstone. He was a missionary to Africa a long time ago. He had multiple issues while he was telling people about God and found it especially difficult to get into the country's central area to spread the Gospel. Another of his issues was his stomach problems. He couldn't handle the water out there to drink, so he bought a goat and drank its milk instead. It was one of the few things he could tolerate.

As time went on, a king from one of the areas where David was preaching came to him and said he wanted David's goat, and replaced it with an old stick. David explains that he was really annoyed at God for allowing this to happen to him. He asked God why when a goat was one of the few things he needed to live. He could only drink goat's milk as his stomach was not good. He needed the goat.

As it turns out, the 'old stick' the king gave him was the king's own rod. When shown at the gate of any community, the community must grant entrance and provide David with all that he needed while he stayed there. David had just been given access to the whole of Africa to spread the Gospel, and all of his needs provided for. All it had cost him was an old goat.

Sometimes in life, it can feel like God has taken what we need and given us something useless in its place. We can get upset and cling to what God is trying to take away from us. We can be angry and ask why. We can converse with God and not understand what He is doing. But God sees the big picture. He knows what we need as opposed to what we think we need. He knows what is helpful as opposed to what we believe is valuable. He knows what is good for us instead of what we believe is good for us.

God knows. .

God is faithful, and nothing He does will ever bring us harm. We may not see it right away, but He may just be opening up an entire kingdom of opportunity to us by taking our goats away. What are you complaining about that God seems to have denied you or taken from you?

Could it be if we dared to wait, if we trusted, and looked at the bigger picture, we might see God's hand at work in our lives for our good and His glory.

Day 14
Dare to Realise

"I AM THE RESURRECTION AND THE LIFE. WHOEVER BELIEVES IN ME, THOUGH HE DIES, YET SHALL HE LIVE."
JOHN 11:25

We have been reading the crucifixion story with Hannah before bed. Tonight, when Jesus was dying on the cross, Hannah said to me, "It's OK mummy, He's still alive, you know."

What a fantastic reminder for us. Jesus is still alive!

The world is a complete mess, and it's getting scarier as we see the news headlines. We can allow ourselves to get worked up and question where God is in the situations we see, or we can remind ourselves, He's still alive! Even when everything around us seems chaotic, even when it seems as though right is wrong and wrong seems right, He's still alive.

That fact is still the same, and it means the Church can keep their heads up and their eyes lifted. It means the Church has a firm foundation when all about it is shaking. The Church can reach out with good news despite the bad we face.

I love Easter time because it allows us to really remind the devil that he has lost and his worst possible outcome for us, death, doesn't even hold a sting anymore. I love reminding the devil of what Jesus did when He died on the cross and rose again. The crucifixion tells the devil that the price for us has been paid in full and the resurrection reminds him of his future so we can sing praise and worship our God because He is worthy. We can firmly believe that we will live, even if we die, because Jesus has conquered death and sin and all that goes along with them in this world.

So today, instead of going to God in prayer with heavy hearts, let's pour our burdens out to a God who is still alive, still in control, still able, still cares, still loves us and still can help. Let us approach God with the realisation that He is alive and He has given us the same Spirit who raised Him from the dead to help us on this journey of life.

Dare to realise the power we have available to us. Not even death, the thing many people fear the most, holds any power against our God. Let us dare to realise that the same power that conquered the grave lives in us today if we are followers of Christ. Let's begin to live that way instead of in fear.

Do not allow your fear to control you, instead let God overwhelm you with His power and dare to realise that because He lives, we can face tomorrow and the next day and every day in our future no matter what comes against us. Jesus is alive.

Day 15
Dare to live

"I AM THE RESURRECTION AND THE LIFE, HE THAT BELIEVETH IN ME, THOUGH HE WERE DEAD, YET SHALL HE LIVE."
JOHN 11:25

I used to be a nurse before God called me into my current position. I loved nursing; It was the job I had waited my whole life to do. I ended up working in the high dependency respiratory ward full of patients facing life or death situations. A lot of the time, we faced death in our ward. Death is brutal to face. One thing I know for sure, however, is that when that person is pronounced dead, they are gone. Their personality is gone, their body systems are gone, they are just a shell. And I saw first hand that to many people death is a hopeless situation and grief can be too much to bear. Death may seem like the end to many people.

However, we have good news in the Gospel that we have received from our Lord Jesus Christ. Jesus said that death does not have to be the end for us. Jesus said that death does not need to be where our journey stops. Good news, amazing news, life-altering news. Can you remember hearing this for the first time? Sometimes we hear this good news so much that we forget how life-altering this actually is. Jesus has turned death itself upside down. When Jesus rose from the dead, He conquered it and so He now is in control of all that happens after death.

Jesus loved us so much that He didn't want to keep His life-giving resurrection power to Himself but gave it to all men and women who follow Him. Death does not have to be the end for you. You can have a life that will never end, that death itself cannot even defeat if you give your life over to Jesus today.

Many people think that 'eternal life' begins after you die. However, the Bible teaches that eternal life begins as soon as you ask Jesus to be your Saviour and turn your life around to follow Him. We are given new purpose, new hope, new meaning, new joy, new life and new prospects when we begin to follow Jesus. We start to live our life with Jesus at the centre instead of us, and because of that we have something worth living for that goes beyond this earthly life and all it offers us.

What a Saviour we have. If you are a believer today, thank our God for this unspeakable gift that He has blessed us with. If you do not follow God yet, today could be your day to give up all and turn your life around and follow Him. You do not have to die spiritually. You can live if you follow the resurrection and the life.

Dare to hope, dare to live, dare to believe, dare to follow Him, and your eternal life will begin here on earth. Thanks be to our God!

Day 16
Dare to dream
**"WRITE THE VISION DOWN AND MAKE IT PLAIN SO HE MAY RUN
WHO READS IT."
HABAKKUK 2:2**

A good few months ago, God gave me a vision. A vision for
praise to be sung aloud in the middle of a village over
Halloween weekend. I went back and forth, wondering if I
should plan something or not.

What if it didn't work out? You don't want to look like a failure.
What if people don't come? That would be a letdown.
What if the weather was wet? It wouldn't work.
I hadn't told anyone about it, so no one would know if it hadn't
happened.

So many questions, many excuses whispered, many possibilities
put in front of me. So many reasons that I could back out of
running with my vision. The devil loves to try and stop you from
running with your vision because he knows God-given vision
has power and potential and can damage his kingdom if it
becomes a reality.

He will give you excuses, obstacles, circumstances, failure, and
anything else that will stop you from putting your idea into
action. The Bible says, "without vision, people perish", (Proverbs
29:18). To obtain ideas from God, it is essential to listen to Him,
read His word and obey His promptings. Once you receive
God's plan, it is vital to put it into action rather than just words in
your life.

If you just listen and do nothing, it would be like sitting inside a
plane on the runway. So much potential, but unless it's put into
action, it's useless. Don't let the devil and his excuses and
possibilities stop you from putting your plan into action. Maybe
tonight, you could sit down and write out your God-given dream
and steps to start seeing it begin. It could be an idea God gave

you to reach workmates, school friends, creative projects, help someone, or build something. Write it down, make it plain and take steps to start it. Sometimes it helps to bring others in on the idea so they can help you keep fighting when you feel like giving up.

That weekend I saw my vision become a reality. And it's incredible when you take a step of faith how God meets you right there with His power and strength. What's stopping you doing something? Take it to God and ask him to help you. Who knows, your dream could become a reality and could help many people find God for themselves, but you have to act!

Dare to dream the plan that God has given to you and it makes your praise and faith so much sweeter when you see it happen.

Day 17
Dare to stand
"THE LORD WILL FIGHT FOR YOU WHILE YOU KEEP STILL."
EXODUS 14:14

It did not feel like we were moving at all! It felt more like we were just suspended in mid-air, albeit 2100 feet up in the air. It was so still and steady that you did not feel like you were floating in a hot air balloon across the country! And yet that is precisely what was happening. By the time we landed, we had floated almost eleven miles across the country, yet it felt like we had hardly moved. The only giveaway was the fields moving below us but had you been looking up, you would have sworn you had floated in the one place.

I hate feeling like I am not moving or going anywhere. I hate feeling stifled and stuck. That frustrates me! But I often do! I often feel like I am not moving, like I am not making an impact, not fulfilling my potential, and like I am not going forward in my walk or ministry. And then I get frustrated!

I can't always see the spiritual side of life! But just like in the balloon, I may be moving far more than I can ever and will ever get to see in the spiritual realm. The reason is that God is fighting for me, carrying me, holding me, has plans for me, has a purpose for me, and wastes nothing that has happened in my life since the day I gave it to Him to use! So even though in the physical, I may get frustrated and feel stuck, in the spiritual, I'm moving more than I ever imagined because God never breaks His promises.

I couldn't have flown that balloon to where it landed. I wouldn't have the first idea of getting it off the ground; I just had to stand there and trust the pilot to take me up and down again. So often, I try to get myself to the next stage of my journey and the next phase of action that God wants for me. We often think we know better and try to tell God what to do instead of actually praying to Him with humility and allowing Him to be fully in control.

God is saying to me, and maybe to you, to stand. As long as I stay where I am meant to be, God will take me on this journey! It might feel like you aren't moving, it might feel scary, it might feel like you are just floating in mid-air waiting to move. God will never let you down.

Dare to stand and let Him carry you, and you will move further and see far more happen than you ever thought you would!

Day 18
Dare to be protected

"HE WILL COVER YOU WITH HIS FEATHERS, AND HE WILL SHELTER YOU WITH HIS WINGS. HIS FAITHFUL PROMISES ARE YOUR ARMOUR AND PROTECTION."
PSALM 91:4

I don't like birds. To say I don't like them is an understatement. I am scared of birds! All birds. The only birds I will allow into my personal space are robins and ducks, and that is purely because my girls love both of them.

I remember a while ago, God gave me pictures of birds and protection every time i read the Bible or every time someone came to speak to me to encourage me. So when I began to feel knocked about by the devil and surrounded on every side by trouble, God reminded me of this verse. Now the thought of being covered with wings made me freak out just a little bit. However, the more I looked into what this meant, I realised what God had told me. He told me I was safe, regardless of what was happening around me.

To me, feathers meant something soft, something defenceless. But actually, bird wings and feathers are their armour and defence mechanisms. A bird wing is like an arm, and it has a shoulder and a wrist and a long arm bone. A feather is strong, and when all together, feathers create a potent force around a defenceless baby chick. Scientists say that the core of a bird's feather is of similar strength to carbon fibre, the material that jet planes are made from! So to say that God surrounds me with His feathers and wings is to say that He has me wholly covered on every side with strength and a force to be reckoned with.

Underneath us and all around us are the wings of God surrounding His defenceless child from every knock and stamp from the evil one. With His wings around us, He takes the brunt of the battle force, so we don't have to. We can just rest underneath the security we feel from Him. Even when the time comes for the baby chicks to learn to fly, the mother bird will swoop under a chick having difficulty and rescue them on her wings, soaring high up with them resting on her strength.

Sometimes we may feel like we are falling or are not able to face what God has set in front of me. The battle can sometimes feel too strong and fierce and we feel unsafe and vulnerable. Let's remember when we have the feeling of vulnerability as a Christian, we do not have to fear the roaring lion because I have the wings of God all around me. Are you feeling unsafe?

Dare to be protected and experience the security of His wings and feathers. He will cover and protect you if you ask.

Day 19
Dare to be covered
"FOR YOU HAVE BEEN MY HELP, AND IN THE SHADOW OF YOUR WINGS, I SING FOR JOY."
PSALM 63:7

Hannah went through a time when she was slightly obsessed with shadows. She loved seeing them move and seeing how they followed you everywhere you went. I've learnt a lot about shadows from watching her watch them. Shadows are dark; they move, they follow, and in Hannah's words, "Mummy, your shadows watching me." But shadows come out when there is light behind them. They don't appear when there is only darkness. There has to be light as well for a shadow to happen.

The Bible talks about the valley of the shadow of death that we will have to experience from time to time. I know from experience that this is a painful shadow that can feel very dark and lonely. You can feel alone and that God has forgotten about you, and isn't listening. Within a shadowy place it can often feel cooler than when you were in the light. We can often feel like we are on the outskirts of God's love and kindness to us when we are in the shadows. We can often feel like God has set us out on the sidelines rather than holding us as close as He can right when we need Him the most.

I want to encourage you, the Light is still there; even within the shadow. God's light is still surrounding you, and this valley is only but a shadow if you're following the One who can protect you through it. It has no power of its own. It has to bow to the One who has defeated death entirely.

So when you are facing this shadow, the Bible refers to another shadow that is as real, present and available to you. The shadow of His Wings- God's Wings, God's presence covering you, surrounding you, championing you and protecting you as you face things you never thought you would have to face. God has not set you apart, He is not watching you from a distance.

He is walking with you through this shadowy valley. He is covering you from attack on every side and He is weeping with you as you face things you hoped you would never have to face.

Shadows. In Hannah's words, "Mummy, your shadow is watching me." God is always watching us, protecting us and covering us as we go through challenging and difficult times. You are not alone, and it is not entirely dark because the light is there. He is the Light of the World, and He will help you through to the other side of the valley; just ask Him to show you the path.

Dare to be covered at your most vulnerable by the One who can protect you the best- God your Saviour.

Day 20
Dare to rest

**"AND THE PEACE THAT SURPASSES ALL UNDERSTANDING WILL
GUARD YOUR HEART AND YOUR MINDS IN CHRIST JESUS."
PHILIPPIANS 4:7**

Jonny and myself have two daughters. As I write this, Hannah is two, and Emily is five months old. As you can imagine, there is not much peace in our house. Peace does not usually enter our vocabulary.

In the past I often heard about today's verse describing "peace that passes understanding," God's peace that just can't be explained or adequately described. However truth be told, I never really had experienced it before, until recently.

After mum died in September 2020, many people asked how we were doing. They were concerned about us as a family losing someone so special, and especially in such a short space of time, just three months since her diagnosis. All I could tell people was that we were experiencing peace. It was not a peace as in nothing is happening in our world, not a peace that explains all is calm. It was a peace that we couldn't explain. A peace that is a bit surreal but real simultaneously, a peace that goes beyond anything the world could offer.

True peace. God given peace that He can provide us with.

We still miss mum terribly. We asked why and cried tears after her death. But there is God in the middle of it all. We experienced what I can only describe as a buffer between us and the real sting of losing mum. A buffer that took the brute force of death. A buffer that is taking the sting out of separation. A buffer that gives us strength beyond what we should have. This verse tells us that we need this peace to guard our hearts and minds. It isn't just to make us feel better, and it isn't just to make us feel peaceful. God knew when we are going through a difficult situation, our hearts and minds would be under attack

41

from the enemy, and we would need a buffer to protect us from the real sting of what is going on.

The buffer, who is God! How amazing is our God that He would do that for us?

Peace is not a word I use much in everyday life. Not an experience I have encountered much. But I have since mum died. If you are experiencing a hard time or dealing with a situation beyond your control, ask God for His peace. Ask people around you to pray for His peace within you.

Only God can give you this peace. We can't find it in the world. We can't find it in other people; We can only find it in Christ Jesus, and when you find it, it makes no real sense and passes all understanding.

Dare to hope in the darkest of situations for peace. Dare to rest in the darkest of circumstances knowing that His peace will protect and hold you. Just ask.

Day 21
Dare to be held

"THE ETERNAL GOD IS YOUR DWELLING PLACE, AND UNDERNEATH ARE THE EVERLASTING ARMS."
DEUTERONOMY 33:27

Emily loves being held. She loves sitting on your knee and being held close. Jonny started to swing her up into the air and back down again, and she laughed and laughed. Why? Because she trusts her father to hold her, protect her, keep her safe, and never let her fall even when she doesn't know what is coming next.

The feeling of being thrown up and down can be scary. But when your Father holds you, you suddenly feel a lot safer and calmer than before, because your Father's arms are one of the safest places to be. Something about the Father's arms gives a sense of security and protection when everything else feels uncertain.

And how incredible is it that God offers us His arms to hold us and protect us when everything about us can seem uncertain and unstable. When everything in front of us looks different from how it looked before, we know that God's arms are still there. When everything around us seems to be dark, we know that God's arms are still there. When we maybe feel more alone than we used to, we can be sure that God's arms are still holding us.

We see many people in the Bible run to the Father's arms when they are in times of trouble. David, Moses, Abraham, Paul, Peter, and even Jesus all ran to the Father's Arms when they faced times of trouble and difficulty yet all in different ways. David wrote songs in order to reach the Father and listen to what He was saying to Him. Moses built the Tabernacle as a way of communicating with God directly. Abraham spoke to God and talked to God about the troubles he was facing in his life. Paul wrote letters to the Church to encourage them and challenge himself, Peter often acted rashly but wanted desperately to

43

follow everything Jesus had taught him and Jesus took Himself off alone and prayed.

We all have different ways of communicating with God to feel the Father's arms around us. Some of us meet Him in worship or praise, some in reading and studying, some in writing or art and some need to be alone, away from everything and everyone to reach and feel the Father's Arms around them.

Today's verse says, "underneath are the everlasting arms" Everlasting. Never changing, never leaving, never-ending, never failing, always there, always near, always holding you and me. So no matter what the pathway ahead looks like to you, be it sickness or lack of finances or family trouble, or even the valley of the shadow of death. The Fathers arms hold you and protect you from every attack the devil may attempt. You just need to call out to Him, and He will be there for you.

Dare to be held by God- the father's arms are what makes all the difference.

Day 22
Dare to Invest
"WHEN I FALL, I SHALL RISE. WHENI SIT IN DARKNESS, THE LORD WILL BE A LIGHT TO ME."
MICAH 7:8

The day before mum received her diagnosis she was at our house for dinner. It was a normal day and we had no idea it would be the last day, before our world was shaken and we were knocked sideways with news we didn't want to hear about a person we thought the world of.

And yet, throughout her illness and even throughout her death, my mum and dad's faith remained unshaken. Even while sitting in the hospital facing an unknown future, one of them said, "God is always good, even when we don't understand, and I hope I will never be angry at Him over anything He decides to do because His plan is perfect." Despite everything that the diagnosis and illness threw at them, their faith remained unshaken.

Why? Because they built their faith up in the good days, because they have seen God prove Himself in the bad days, and because they have a relationship with Him themselves and have got to know who He is. They invested intentionally in their faith throughout the good and bad days, the everyday journey they have walked, their faith was able to carry them through this massive trial they were facing.

I want to encourage us all, myself included, to learn from this example and invest intentionally in your faith now. In the good days, in the ordinary days, in the days when you feel like you could do it yourself -that is the time to invest in your faith. Read your Bible, pray, spend time getting to know God and His character in the ordinary days. That investment will carry you through when you face the hard times, the difficult days, and the horrible facts that make you want to run.

We can only lean on what we know when hard times hit. We can read the Bible when difficulties rise but often our minds are so overwhelmed by what is going on that we cannot take in all that God can offer us. The investment of daily devotionals now will help you rise when you fall and see the light when it is darkest.

I watched mum and dad read and pray daily together and separately, and it was that consistent daily faith-building that carried them through. Not a quick call on God when they face trouble, but a consistent lifestyle that becomes part of who they are. And I encourage us all to do the same.

We may find hard times get a lot easier to face if we know God better before we meet them. If you dare to invest now, you can be unshakeable then.

Day 23
Dare to rely
"HIS NAME SHALL BE CALLED WONDERFUL COUNSELLOR, MIGHTY GOD, EVERLASTING FATHER, PRINCE OF PEACE."
ISAIAH 9:6

Have you had one of "those" days? We all have them. Nothing was going smoothly one morning in our home, we have had a few accidents, and it was only 2pm, still a few hours to bedtime when we all wouldn't sleep again because of colds and teething!. My anxiety and stress level had been pretty high all day by this stage.

It got me thinking about all the people who have "those days" every day. Whose anxiety is constantly through the roof, who have continuous stress and feel under constant pressure. Maybe it's family pressure, financial pressure or mental illness, but they live in a continual state of "those days" with no end in sight.

That must be exhausting!

Today, I want to tell you that if that is you, you're not alone. The isolation and fear that you feel may seem real, but it is a lie. Feelings are natural and God-given, but they are also not to be trusted and can trip us up, making us believe that we are alone, rejected, and unworthy of help.

I want to tell you that there is someone available to you. Someone who can help you through every day, not just 'those days.' His name is Jesus. He is a counsellor, a mighty protector, a friend, a supporter, a healer and a constant companion all in one. He is here for you, for everyone. For people who have days where they feel like they have so much stress and anxiety and hopelessness that sometimes they really can't see a path through.

For people who feel like they have it all together.

Dare to hope

For people who feel like they have no way out.
For people who feel like they have the best life possible.

Jesus is here for you. Hope begins when you realise you have a light in the darkness and support in isolation. Jesus is your hope and help.

You are not alone, and you are not hopeless. You can have Jesus. Those days- Jesus came to help us through those days. He still can. You only have to call out to Him.

Dare to rely on the One who can help you no matter what you face- He will always be there for you.

Day 24
Dare to Ask

"THAT YOU MAY TELL IN THE HEARING OF YOUR SON AND OF YOUR GRANDSON HOW I HAVE DEALT HARSHLY WITH THE EGYPTIANS AND WHAT SIGNS I HAVE DONE AMONG THEM, THAT YOU MAY KNOW THAT I AM THE LORD."
EXODUS 10:2

I frequently pray some pretty big prayers to God. Sometimes I think that I'm crazy for praying them, but I keep praying them because deep down, I believe that God can do what I'm asking if it is His will, even if it seems impossible to me. That's what I love about God. He is able to leave us astounded with the impossible.

I love today's verse. It gets me excited. I want to be able to tell my children and my grandchildren about the signs and wonders that God has done in my life. I want to say to them that God showed us things beyond our imagination. I want to tell them that I believed God enough to pray big prayers that seemed impossible to anyone but God.

Sometimes, we can make God small and make God's power and promises limited, and we can settle for being a slave to the enemy. We sometimes get a thought pattern that means we will accept anything the enemy throws at us because we don't truly believe God is able.

Today, I believe that I will tell my children and grandchildren what God will do in my life, not just what I'm praying about today but also in the future. I don't want to settle for limited slave-like lifestyles, but I want to be able to tell that God is the Lord because of the signs and wonders I've seen Him do in my life.

Are you with me? Are you prepared to start praying big prayers because you want to see that God is Lord? Are you bored living a limited life that doesn't see God's promises and power at work? It takes work and effort. It took Moses ten times of going back and forward against the enemy before he saw his freedom. It may take us time to break free, but in doing so, we will know that He is the Lord.

It may not work out the way you thought or intended. I'm sure Moses expected freedom the first time he visited Pharaoh, or the second, or third, but he didn't. God had a different plan. But no matter what, God will show you His power and promises, if you choose to believe instead of choosing to settle. Don't stop, don't settle. Let's start seeing God's power and work in your life.

Dare to ask this week so that you can tell your children and grandchildren what you have seen God do in your life. God is still the same today as he was in Moses day. What do you want to share with your children? Start praying for it now!

Day 25
Dare to Whisper
"WHEN THE RIGHTEOUS CRY FOR HELP, THE LORD HEARS AND DELIVERS THEM OUT OF ALL THEIR TROUBLES."
PSALM 34:17

Hannah is loud and getting louder. She loves to talk and chat away and loves to shout to ensure that she is heard. However, she will whisper to me every so often to see if I'm listening to her. She does it, especially if I seem distracted. She will sit and whisper, and when she sees that I've heard her, she is so happy, because even if I seem busy, I still listen to her.

How often do we think that our Heavenly Father is too busy or distracted to listen to us? And so we often don't talk to Him or tell Him things or ask for something because we have in our heads He is too distracted by the big things of the world to hear our cry. The Bible says we have not because we ask not, (James 4:2).

David knew that faith in God does not make anyone immune from difficulty (Psalm 34:19). However David, who wrote this Psalm, knew firsthand how God listens to our prayers. God protected David from Goliath (1 Samuel 17:45–51) and from King Saul who chased him in the wilderness (1 Samuel 23:15) because David prayed to God before he made a move.

If you are facing something today that makes you anxious, concerned, fearful or brings tears to your eyes. Sometimes we feel like we cannot raise a shout to God because of the outside pressures coming on your life. Maybe all you can manage today is a whisper, a few words to a God who hears you.

I'd encourage you today to let God hear your whisper, and He will listen to you. There's rarely a time I don't hear Hannah because she is my daughter, and my ear is trained to listen to her. We are God's children, and His ear is trained to hear even the faintest whisper from us about the smallest things. He loves to hear us because it shows Him that we trust Him, want to include Him, and depend on Him.

Dare to whisper your concerns to Him today and see the difference it makes in your world, knowing that the King of Heaven listens to your faintest cry. You are so important to Him.

Day 26
Dare to try

"BEHOLD, I AM DOING A NEW THING, NOW IT SPRINGS FORTH, DO YOU NOT PERCEIVE IT?"
ISAIAH 43:19

Hannah has now been at nursery for almost eight weeks. It's nearly half-term, and she has loved her first term so far. However, a few weeks ago, her teacher pulled me aside and told me she had a minor issue—nothing major, life-changing, or dramatic, just a problem within herself.

As a mummy, I immediately wanted to fix it for her, but there wasn't anything I could do. I just stood by and encouraged her every day to help her overcome it. Today was a breakthrough day, and we overcame what was holding her back, and I've never been prouder. As a mummy, I wanted to fix the battle for her. Part of me knew that if she managed to achieve this for herself, it would be much better for her and bring her out the other side a stronger person.

We sometimes wonder why God lets us go through tricky, complicated or challenging situations in life. We wonder why He isn't stepping in and fixing it for us. We wonder when it will end and what the point of it all is.

Could it be that God is standing back, encouraging you every day until you get your breakthrough? Could it be that God knows this situation you're facing will help you come forth as gold, as it says in the book of Job? Gold isn't just found. Gold comes from dirt that has gone through many processes until it is new. It's dug for, and it's washed. It's hard work until gold comes from the earth.

God wants to strip back issues in our life that are not helping our walk with God. He wants to create a new Spirit within us that will help us do His will in this world. To do that we need to go through a God-process that will not harm us, but help move us forward to have a new relationship, and a new communication with God like we have never had before.

So I want to encourage you. God hasn't forgotten you and isn't letting you go through this process for no reason. God always has our good at heart.

You maybe feel like you have been in a stripping back process for a long time, your breakthrough day may be closer than you think, so keep going! Who knows, but there may be a celebration in Heaven like we had today when a breakthrough is achieved! Hannah's breakthrough made me so proud, and your breakthrough will please God's heart too.

Dare to try. God is with you, for you and wants you to make it.

Day 27
Dare to Wonder
**"I PRAISE YOU FOR I AM FEARFULLY AND WONDERFULLY MADE."
PSALM 139:14**

We have started learning Bible verses each night. Our first verse was, "I am fearfully and wonderfully made." As Hannah repeated the verse, the words changed to "I am carefully made and wonderful."

While I am not one for changing the words of the Bible, how true is this in childhood language? You are carefully made and wonderful. I just wanted to encourage you tonight as you look in the mirror and see your flaws or as you sit at the end of the day and revisit your mistakes. As you sit and watch social media at all those who seem to have it more together than you do.

You have maybe had words spoken to you that are not helpful or true. You may have been told that you're a mistake, or you were not planned. You maybe have thought that this world would be better if you were not in it or that you are so alone that no one even knows you are here.

I want to encourage you and tell you the truth- the Bible truth. What God Himself has said about you in His Word.

You're not a mistake, and you're not an error. You're not on your own. God made you the way you are on purpose for a purpose. He has a plan for you, the very fact you are on this planet today means He wants to use you and has a reason for you being here! He didn't make a mistake, and He didn't forget something. He didn't leave anything out. when He created you The words in today's verse do not just mean 'made', as in carelessly, put together. These words mean that you were fashioned, planned, created, put together with thought and with power and on purpose.

In a world where everyone is obsessed with how they look, how they appear and how other people perceive them, know that God knows you inside and out, and when He looks at you, He says His creation is 'very good.'

You are carefully made and wonderful. And as Hannah says, "The Bible is true, so I must be", and so that means you are too.

Dare to wonder at how beautiful God's creation is and remember that you are part of it, and nothing He has created is ever a mistake.

Day 28
Dare to be faithful
"ONE WHO IS FAITHFUL IN A VERY LITTLE IS ALSO FAITHFUL IN MUCH."
LUKE 16:10

Some days it seems as though all I do is small things. Making lunch, clearing dishes, washing clothes, bedtime kisses, night cuddles. A lot of my life seems minor at the moment. I wonder if you ever feel like God may mean you to live a bigger life than you currently are, but your circumstances seem small and insignificant. Today's verse encourages us to be faithful in the small things.

It was just an ordinary day when Samuel anointed David to be King of Israel, a massive moment that declared to all around him that he would be the most important ruler. I am sure David maybe thought his life had completely changed at that moment, however, he went back to looking after the sheep. There he stayed for another fifteen years or so. Even though God had stated his life would be valuable and influential right now, it stayed small.

One insignificant day, David wandered to a battlefield to deliver lunch. While everyone else was fighting and essential and making a difference, David took a break from watching sheep and delivered lunch. In his eyes, that would be the most he achieved that day. And it was in this small act that God paved the way for David to be raised in God's Kingdom.

I'm sure he felt insignificant and underwhelmed. I'm sure he thought he was capable of more. Little did he know in the lunch delivery that he would conquer a giant. David freed Israel, and David's journey of being a giant in God's kingdom began. Not because he trained in combat; not because the king called him, not because he stopped doing what he thought didn't matter. But because he stayed faithful in the small. He defeated Goliath because he looked after sheep. He was there at the right time because he delivered lunch.

So I encourage you to stay faithful, even in the littlest things in life. If you are a parent, stay faithful because you don't know what the example you leave with your child may lead to. If you're a singer, stay faithful because you don't know where your next song may take someone. If you're a writer, stay faithful because you don't know how your next blog might help someone. If you're a labourer, stay faithful because you don't know who you may meet at your next job.

But it will only happen if we stay faithful. Stay prayerful. Stay looking up to God. Stay focused on what He has given you to do at this moment.

Daring to be faithful in the small can lead to conquering giants if you trust God.

Day 29
Dare to Speak

THEN YOU WILL CALL UPON ME AND COME AND PRAY TO ME, AND I WILL HEAR YOU.
JEREMIAH 29:12

Like many churches, at the beginning of each year our church enters into a period of prayer and fasting, taking time to listen and tune into what God wants to say for the upcoming year. It's such a good spiritual exercise to get in the habit of starting a new year.

So many times, I hear people say that they don't know how to pray correctly. They think that unless they use "proper terms" or "right language", their prayers are somehow inadequate or less valuable or lack strength compared to others. And so they stay silent in prayer meetings and they do not raise their cry to God because they feel like their prayer will be so insignificant compared to others.

Yesterday Hannah brought me a picture of her first attempt at writing "Mummy". To some people, it was a 'put in the bin' scribble. To me, it is precious. Not just because it is a first writing attempt, but because of the heart behind the scribble.

She brought it to me, saying, "I wrote this for you, mummy, because I love you." I couldn't care if she misspelt it, if she didn't get it all in the one line, or if the "Y" was funny looking. The heart behind it means it is so unique and precious to me.

God doesn't need formal language used in prayer. He doesn't necessarily need the right words or proper terms. God needs a right heart for prayer. A heart that comes to speak to Him because they love Him. A heart that knows He can do all things, so prayers are spoken with that attitude. A heart that worships Him because they owe Him everything.

That's what God needs. A prayer with all the right words with the right heart, or a prayer stumbled through with wrong words and misplaced sentences with a right heart, is one of the most precious things that God hears. God loves to hear your voice come to Him in prayer to bring Him into your day. The right heart makes the difference.

So take heart and dare to speak up in prayer to God. He will turn His ear to you, and I can only imagine His heart when He hears your 'scribbled prayer', as it were because you love Him.

Day 30
Dare to Stay Beside
"KEEP STEADY MY STEPS, ACCORDING TO YOUR PROMISE."
PSALM 119:133

We went to the beach a while ago, along with what seemed like half of Northern Ireland! There were so many surfers in the water catching the big waves. Some were loving it, some ran in and ran out again. The waves hit, and if you were on the smaller side, you needed someone beside you to hold you and keep you steady.

Emily, our youngest daughter who was one at the time, didn't quite realise this and made a quick attempt to get into the water by herself. She didn't realise she needed to stay with her father to keep her from the waves that could hit her. She didn't realise entering the water on her own could lead to her being swept out and into danger.

But she was safe with her father by her side (or holding on to her hood). Her father could take the brunt of any waves that hit. Her father could hold onto her if a wave caught her off guard and toppled her over. Even though the waves attempted to produce fear and unease, the father provides protection and safety.

Maybe where you are standing today feels a bit uncertain, perhaps there are waves of doubt or fear coming toward you, and you think you have no one to hold onto. It could be easy to feel fearful as we look into the unknown. We don't necessarily realise that with our Father God by our side, we can be confident and protected and hopeful because the Father can take the brunt of anything we may face. Our Father by our side prevents any wave of danger, fear, or uncertainty from taking us out. They may hit us, but they will not overwhelm us because our Father has promised us so.

On the other hand, we may not realise we need the Father as we face life alone. Many of us think we can do it ourselves, as Emily did. We don't quite see how vulnerable we are without the Father beside us. Maybe today, before you live to see another day, you could realise how essential it is for the Father to be beside you so that you're not facing it on your own. You have protection, power, support, and help with the Father beside you. Maybe today, you could allow the Father God to break into your life and be your Saviour, so you don't have to face life alone.

You can begin to live with the Father beside you - helping you, supporting you through any waves of life you may face, protecting you against storms that may come your way.

Dare to stay beside, hold his hand, and He will be right with you throughout every wave that breaks against you.

Day 31
Dare to Endure

"WE REJOICE IN OUR SUFFERINGS, KNOWING THAT SUFFERING PRODUCES ENDURANCE, AND ENDURANCE PRODUCES CHARACTER, AND CHARACTER PRODUCES HOPE."
ROMANS 5:3-4

Endurance- 'The ability to suffer a difficult process or situation without giving way."

Hannah started nursery this year. If you are a parent, you will understand the difficult task of letting your child go and handing them over to another person. It is all well and good and feels like a holiday until your child hits a problem, something in their wee world at school that you cannot fix. Until now, you have been their number one go-to on all things difficult, so the fact that you cannot fix it for them is a challenge. They must go this one alone. It is hard to watch, challenging to see them struggle until they manage it.

Then you see something you have never seen before. A new element of your child emerges. A part of them had never had to rise before because parents did everything for them. This part is new, confident, self-assured, and proud of themselves for having achieved a small battle in their world, leading to a forever change in their character. Much as we would have wanted to have fought the battle for them, sometimes this new change is for the better and the long term, helping them in their adult lives as they go on.

Paul here says to rejoice in our sufferings; why? Not because they are fun, not because they are exciting or add a new spin on life. But because of the fruit that it produces for us. God does not stand back and watch us in our suffering for the fun of it, or to give Him something to do. Believe me, as a parent, I can only imagine how it breaks God's heart to watch His very much loved child suffering. However, just as Hannah gets the chance to conquer and develop a new side to her character, God allows us that chance in our lives.

We can gain endurance in our lives, which will last forever. In the future, when we hit a difficulty, we know that God can and will help us stick at it because He has done it before, and we will learn how important that quality is.

We get the chance to gain new qualities in our character that has never been seen before. The fruit of the Spirit that is love, joy, peace, patience, kindness, goodness, faithfulness, gentleness, and self-control all are developed because of endurance in our lives, which comes from suffering, as today's verse tells us.

And from those new traits, we find hope. We have a deep-rooted hope that whatever we face in the future will be for our good because God never lets anything happen that is not. We get the hope that God will be beside us because He was before. We get the hope that we can endure because we did before. This hope cannot be shifted or taken away from us because it is now a deep-rooted part of our character because of the suffering we faced. So if you are going through suffering, hold your head up and rise to the challenge. You will look back someday and see all the traits, characters, and hope that developed because of what you face today.

Dare to endure. God is there, He will help, and He will allow you to develop new spiritual traits because He loves you so.

Day 32
Dare to Weep
"JESUS WEPT"
JOHN 11:35

I remember our first Christmas without mum. It was not the day itself that made me think of her the most that year or any year since. It was the decorations. Mum loved the Christmas decorations. I remember her telling me she would buy herself something new for the house every year and advising me to build up my decorations by doing the same thing. And so, when it came to decorating my home, memories rose that I was not expecting.

It made me wonder as I was sitting giving Emily her bottle in the darkness that night if Jesus understood the feeling of loss. I always knew he understood how we felt, but had he ever felt what we feel? Not just the feeling of losing someone; we all know He did because He lost friends and family while He was alive. I mean the stabbing, unrelenting pain of grief that comes over you when you lose someone. Part of me wondered if He had ever felt that pain because He understands what happens after death, so surely that side of loss would not affect Him.

Then I remember two words in the darkness, "Jesus wept."

At the grave of one of his closest friends, Lazarus, Jesus wept. Jesus heard. Jesus experienced. Jesus understands. Jesus felt. Jesus cares. I know so many people who have had a loss in their lives. They lost their parents, lost their health, lost their spouses, lost a friend, lost a baby, lost a job, lost a home, lost hope. You have all felt loss in your life in some way. Maybe you have been wondering if Jesus understands or if Jesus cares.

Jesus wept.

I am fully convinced at that moment that God the Father allowed Jesus to feel all that we feel when death and loss occur in our lives, so that the Bible could genuinely say He is fully acquainted with all our ways. So that Jesus can help us when we feel loss and pain in our lives because He has been there too. He has experienced it, and He understands it.

God, Himself, takes us by the hand and leads us out of that pain, not just because He is God, but because He knows the way through and has passed through it Himself. Thank God He understands because it means we are not alone when facing the valley of the shadow of death. God says to you, "I am with you always," Matthew 28:20.

If you feel a stab of pain at a loss you have experienced today, take heart, dare to weep and know that your Saviour is in it with you because He has gone through it Himself. He will hold your hand until you make it through.

Day 33
Dare to fight

**"AND I LOOKED AND AROSE AND SAID TO THE NOBLES AND TO THE OFFICIALS AND TO THE REST OF THE PEOPLE, "DO NOT BE AFRAID OF THEM. REMEMBER THE LORD WHO IS GREAT AND AWESOME AND FIGHT FOR YOUR BROTHERS, YOUR SONS, YOUR DAUGHTERS, YOUR WIVES AND YOUR HOMES."
NEHEMIAH 4:14**

A while ago, I had a fight on my hands. Our daughter had a chest infection and conjunctivitis with a constant temperature of 38.7 for three days. The nurse in me knew what it was and what she needed. She needed antibiotics for both her eyes and her chest. However, my GP disagreed and told me it was a virus.

I am not one to run for an antibiotic for every illness I experience, but I knew our daughter needed one this time. So the nurse and the mummy in me fought for what I knew she needed. I didn't want to sit back and let the infection overtake my baby when I knew the remedy. And my 'fighting' paid off with an antibiotic for both her chest and eyes. And within 24 hours, she was a different child.

Sometimes in life, we have to fight for what matters and not sit back and accept second-hand information. We need to follow our gut instinct and decide what we know is important enough not to back down.

Nehemiah had to do this. He had rallied the whole of Israel to rebuild the walls of Jerusalem. He had got them in position. He had given them their slot, and the work had begun. And then the voices started. You know the voices that will always put you down no matter what you do. No matter how much you succeed, the voices will always try to humiliate you—the enemy voice. And the people and the work stopped.

Nehemiah had a choice. He could allow the people and the work to stop and listen to the enemy's voice too. Or he could fight for what matters.

God had given him a vision, a purpose, and the enemy was threatening to stop it. So he fought. He reminded the people not to fear amidst the confusion. He reminded them of their awesome God, who had never failed them and never would. He reminded them of God's power and plan. Nehemiah urged them to fight along with him. He reminded them of why they were doing this hard work, "Fight for your families. Fight for your brother, your sons, your daughters, your wives and your homes." Fight for what matters. And they did.

They completed the work because some things in life are worth fighting for, no matter your personality type.

So I entice you and encourage you to fight for what matters. When something threatens your spiritual life- Confusion, enemy voices, distraction, something that seems too hard, too slow, insignificant-fight. Fight for your families, your homes and your spiritual walk with God. The Church has become very good at lying down and praying to God, essential. But there comes the point when it is our responsibility to fight.

I encourage you to take a spiritual health check. Stop the insignificant battles that so many of us are engaged in and start to fight for what is important. God will meet you in the struggle and see the work flourish because we did our part.

Dare to fight for what matters, and together we can stop listening to those outside voices and see the kingdom of God built.

Day 34
Dare to Rise Up

THEN I LOOKED AND AROSE AND SAID TO THE NOBLES AND TO THE OFFICIALS AND TO THE REST OF THE PEOPLE, "DO NOT BE AFRAID OF THEM. REMEMBER THE LORD WHO IS GREAT AND AWESOME AND FIGHT FOR YOUR BROTHERS, YOUR SONS, YOUR DAUGHTERS, YOUR WIVES AND YOUR HOMES."
NEHEMIAH 4:14

There is a tactic that the devil loves to use to get us to stop the work that God has given us to do. It is a tactic as old as time itself, yet it often works among God's people. So usually, when God's work begins to take off, your vision begins to take ground, and you start to see God's promise in your life come to pass, the devil will swoop in with his age-old tactic of discouragement to stop you in your tracks.

The devil hates to see God's work begin, so if he can get in among your thinking, distract you with discouragement, and get you to doubt what God has told you will happen, it will help prevent the work from going any further. Nehemiah encountered this just as the walls of Jerusalem were beginning to be built. Nehemiah had gathered the people altogether, he had told them his vision, he had gained their enthusiasm for what he was doing, and he had delegated each man a section of the wall to build. It all seemed to be going so well.

Then the voices came. Those voices of people who don't understand what you are doing, those voices of negativity and doubt, those voices of people who want to see you fail and are happiest when other people fall. Those voices. They always seem to appear just as the work is getting going. We have all heard them, haven't we?

What did Nehemiah do? He could have sat down and given up. He could have listened and taken in all they were saying. He could have agreed with them and told the people to go home.

He could have accepted discouragement and doubt and drove the vision into the ground. But. I love that there is a but among God's people. But they didn't. Nehemiah decided his God-given vision was too important. He decided that God was worth listening to above anyone else. He decided to keep going despite the circumstances around him. The Bible says Nehemiah looked and arose. He rose. Over the negativity, he rose. Over the doubt, he rose. Over discouragement, he rose. Over the debates, he rose. He rose because he knew God was more important. He rose because he knew his passion was vital. He rose because he knew building this kingdom would impact the world. He rose.

And because he rose, people got back to work and followed his lead.

Today, do you need to decide to rise? Maybe discouragement, doubt, negativity, and jealousy have made you sit down and give up recently. Today I encourage you to rise. Nothing in Nehemiah's circumstances changed. The voices were still there. Despite all that was going on around him, he needed to rise and decide who he would listen to.

Today I encourage you to dare to rise again. Listen to God's voice above all others. Renew your God-given vision in your mind. Read God's promises again and rise to the place where God has called you and intended you to be. Rise against the devil's tactics to keep you down. Use God's word against him and remind him of your position in Christ. This world needs a Church of God who will rise despite what is happening around them. Will that be you?

Day 35
Dare to be fearless

**THEN I LOOKED AND AROSE AND SAID TO THE NOBLES AND TO THE OFFICIALS AND TO THE REST OF THE PEOPLE, "DO NOT BE AFRAID OF THEM. REMEMBER THE LORD WHO IS GREAT AND AWESOME AND FIGHT FOR YOUR BROTHERS, YOUR SONS, YOUR DAUGHTERS, YOUR WIVES AND YOUR HOMES."
NEHEMIAH 4:14**

We have a park just behind our house. It is convenient to take the girls around to when we are all getting a bit of cabin fever. In that park is a rope bridge. It is a criss-cross bit of rope you have to try and walk across from one edge to the other. When Hannah was starting to go around the park independently, she could do everything except that bridge. There was something about that bridge that scared her. It is not a scary bridge on its own, but when you are a two-year-old with feet that could go through the holes, you can understand why fear would strike. I remember the first day Hannah conquered that fear and walked across it. I was so proud of her. It was slow, but she did it. I was never far away, but she did it. The fact that she conquered her fear made me so proud of her.

Nehemiah was trying to rally the troops to keep going on the wall, despite the voices and people planting doubt within them. "Do not be afraid of them", he cried out to the people. Fear. Fear can be debilitating. It is an enemy to confidence in what you are about to do. It can mean the difference between making a difference in this world and sitting on the sidelines. Fear can seem very real to us even though the world looking in cannot see what is so scary.

I wonder if something in your life stops you from fulfilling your God-given role in this world because you feel fear. Every time you do what you know you should do, that thing, that voice, that person, that doubt, that fear rises again and pushes you back. Is there something preventing you from reaching the path God intends for you?

The antidote to fear is given to us in this verse. Nehemiah proclaimed, do not be afraid, not because the circumstances had changed, not because people had gone, not because the walls were already finished. Nehemiah declared not to fear, but "remember the Lord who is great and awesome". The antidote to the fear you feel? Remember the Lord who is stronger than anything in your way, who is greater than any fear you face, who is more awesome than any negative word spoken against you. Remember the Lord who can carry you through this challenge. Remember, the Lord is on your side. Remember the Lord who knows you by name. Remember the Lord who loves you and cares for you. Remember the Lord who gave you this vision and knows you can do it. Remember the Lord who created you to do this very task. Remember the Lord.

Maybe today, you need to remember the Lord in your circumstances. Perhaps you need to get into His Word and remember why you started. Perhaps you need to remember who He is and why He called you. Maybe you need to sit and remember so you can dare to be fearless in what He has called you to do.

You can make a difference in this world if you dare to be fearless. Fearlessness is not a lack of fear; it is doing what God has called you to do despite fear. You can remember the Lord, and you will see the difference that makes in your fight for Him.

Day 36
Dare to be searched

"SEARCH ME, O GOD, AND KNOW MY HEART....AND SEE IF THERE BE ANY GRIEVOUS WAY IN ME AND LEAD ME IN THE WAY EVERLASTING."
PSALM 139:23-24

We have all been there. You have carefully packed your suitcase and put everything where you want it. You set it on the security belt, and it goes through the scanner. All is going well until it comes out the other side, and the security guy picks your bag up and sets it to the side. Belts and shoes come off, bags get ripped open, all to be searched. Among this all happening, you also set the security alarm off when you walked through the scanner and now have to be searched as well. We all feel a bit vulnerable when we are being searched. No one looks forward to being searched and having someone else rooting through our things. It is personal to us, exposing us even if we have nothing to hide. We want to keep some things private.

In the Psalms we see David actually crying out to God to search him and know his heart. He wanted to be exposed to God, to be vulnerable before him, to lay all his mess out before our God. Why? Because David realised that, although being searched can make you feel vulnerable and exposed, it will lead to a deeper, closer relationship with God in the long term. We can only gain a deep connection if we allow God to deal with anything that stands between Him and us.

When was the last time we exposed ourselves to such a thorough search? The kind of search that allows our deepest secrets to be revealed. The type of search that makes us feel a bit uncomfortable and brings things up that we want to forget. God does not do this to embarrass us or make us feel uncomfortable. God searches us to get rid of stuff He knows is standing between us and life in all its fullness. God searches us to get rid of things preventing Him from using us to our fullest potential.

However, unlike security at the airport, God never imposes this search. God never pulls you up in front of everyone and starts pulling out our most private thoughts before the world to see. God waits. He waits for us to invite Him to search. He waits for us to allow Him to enter our most private places in our lives. Gently but thoroughly, He begins to declutter those things in there that prevent us from that most profound relationship we can have with Him.

It may be uncomfortable, but it is so worth it. Are you willing to allow God, the Father who loves you, to have this access today? You may be wondering why your relationship with God isn't where it once was, or why you are not experiencing life in all its fullness as the Bible promised.

Just maybe, if you dare to be searched, you may find it gives you a spiritual makeover you have never experienced before. But you have to invite Him to do it first!

Day 37
Dare to Accept
"MALE AND FEMALE HE (GOD) CREATED THEM. AND GOD BLESSED THEM."
GENESIS 1:27B-28

In today's society, it can be so easy to believe the lie that unless you are married with two children, a picket fence and a dog, you are not blessed. So often, I have heard people say that 'they never knew love until they became a parent' or 'I never started living until I was married.' It can be so easy to fall into the trap of believing that unless you have what society deems essential to living a full life, you are missing out. There is always something more that seems to be required, and no matter what you have, the goalposts constantly seem to be moved.

I love this verse in Genesis. Right at the beginning of our Bible, God tells us who we are. It says God created man and woman and blessed them.

God created you on purpose for a purpose. The life you have, the family you have, the place you were born, the siblings you have were all intended by God for you to have. You are not a mistake. You are not a group of cells formed together randomly. God created you.

Dare to accept who you are without anything else attached to you. You do not need to be married to matter; you were created by God, which means you matter already. You do not need to have children to have value; God created you, which means you matter already. You do not need to have your own home, the best job, the best car to be of value; you were created by God, which means you matter as you are.

God has blessed you as He created you. Married, you are blessed. Unmarried, you are blessed. Children, you are blessed. No children, you are blessed. With a great job, you are blessed.

Without a job, you are blessed. You are blessed right where you are by a God who knows what He is talking about.

Of course, we can always do things to improve our situation. We can always make life better for ourselves, but you do not need to improve anything in your life for you to matter to God or to be blessed by God. You already are.

So today, dare to accept that you are created, and that you are blessed. When you realise that it will impact how you live your life and what you aim for in your world. You are made and blessed by the God of the Universe who rules over all things.

Day 38
Dare to Progress
"HE WHO BEGAN A GOOD WORK IN YOU WILL BRING IT TO COMPLETION."
PHILIPPIANS 1:6

We did a complete renovation of our living room not so long ago. My husband finished it beautifully. That is often when people see the product when it is completed. Not many people saw it when it was a complete mess, an inch of dust everywhere, and we had to search for everything we wanted because the house was upside down. Many of us like Instagram pictures, but we don't like the process of getting there. It can be a hard slog, painful and intense. The Instagram finish is much more attractive than the effort.

In our spiritual lives, it can feel so much like that. We want the complete picture, not the steps God brings us along to enhance our growth and our relationship with him. We don't always like the process God can bring into our lives when something needs to be changed, or we need to move forward.

There were many times I wished I could click my fingers and jump over a process God was bringing me through. It often felt messy, intense and demanding. And yet the place it brought me to was so much better than where I was before.

There is a verse that says, when I have been refined, I shall come forth as gold (Job 23:10). Refining to become gold sounds like a great promise. But the process isn't glamourous. Gold is heated until it melts which is at a really high temperature, and the dirt and mess within it comes to the surface. The dirt then has to be cleaned. The process is dirty, hot and challenging, but you're left with gold, pure gold.

If it feels like you're in the middle of an arduously intense process, keep going. The mess can be good. The process can mean change is coming, and God is working and moving you into another level with Him. Progress is always hard work but it always helps lead to something new. Steps are hard work but they lead you to a new level.

Dare to progress in your spiritual walk. Change is hard, but the result brings something you could never reach on your own- A deeper relationship with God. That is something worth fighting for.

Day 39
Dare to have confidence

"LET US THEN WITH CONFIDENCE DRAW NEAR TO THE THRONE OF GRACE THAT WE MAY RECEIVE MERCY AND FIND GRACE TO HELP IN TIME OF NEED."
HEBREWS 4:16

I can still picture the long hallway in our home when I was three years old. I remember getting up after a bad dream and heading up the hall to my parent's bedroom. That is where you instinctively go whenever you need someone to help you. You know that whatever you are facing, thinking about, trying to get through, your parents are the people you can turn to for help, support, relief and courage. Your parents are the people you look for, even as you get older.

I often remember my dad walking me back down the hall to my bed and praying with me while tucking me back in. Nothing had changed; my circumstances were the same-it was still dark, quiet, and I was alone, but my dad was there beside me, which made all the difference.

This verse encourages us to approach God's throne in our time of need so we may find help, grace, support and courage to face whatever it is we are facing. It does not say that God will remove what we are facing; it says He will help us.

There is a clear difference in this. Often, we want God to remove the circumstances, and when He does not, we begin to lose faith. Have we done something wrong? Does He not love us enough? Do we not have enough faith in God? God did not say He would change our circumstances; He said He would help us, and that is where we can draw our confidence.

While our circumstances may not change, we now have Heaven's help, support, and power available to us if we draw near to God. I am so thankful I can have confidence that the

God of Heaven has promised to help me in every circumstance I find myself in.

Maybe you are facing something right now and you don't fully understand the reason. Trust God now as much as you did when times were good. Believe in Him now as much as you did before. He is always good, always for you and always with you, even if it doesn't feel like it.

Make a choice. Dare to have confidence that God's help is at hand. It helps change your perspective on everything you're facing when you choose to trust.

Day 40
Dare to Witness

"AND THERE IS SALVATION IN NO ONE ELSE, FOR THERE IS NO OTHER NAME UNDER HEAVEN GIVEN AMONG MEN BY WHICH WE MUST BE SAVED."
ACTS 4:12

Hannah loves her big sister role. She especially loves taking Emily by the hand and leading her where she should go. One morning, coming out of the kid's church, in the middle of a crowded corridor, Hannah grabbed Emily's hand and said, "Come with me, Emily. I will show you the right way to go."

I love her passion for showing Emily the right way to go and the right path to take. She feels responsible for her little sister to ensure she isn't lost, isn't forgotten, or left behind. Because Hannah knows the pathway, she can lead those coming behind her.

If you know Jesus, you know the right pathway and the right way to lead people. It doesn't take someone who has been to Bible College to lead people to Jesus; it doesn't take someone who has read their Bible through each year or who knows all the right words to say. It takes someone who has had an encounter with Jesus and got right with God themselves, because they have experienced it for themselves.

Hannah doesn't know the whole of our church building. She doesn't know how it is financed or where you go to get a cup of coffee. But she knows the pathway that Emily needs to take.

You may feel like you don't know all the intricate details of God or everything the Bible says about Him. But you know how to get to God and what others need to do to make it to Him. Those you love need to know, so they aren't lost, forgotten, or left behind.

Jesus promised before He left this world that if we would have power from Heaven to help us tell others the truth and the way to get to Jesus. You may feel uncomfortable the first time you try to tell someone the truth. You may get your words twisted and your stomach may feel in a knot. Don't let that stop you from speaking up. Your friends and family in your world need to know the truth about how to reach Jesus. You are in their world for a reason. God needs you to tell them the way, even if you don't feel adequate for the job.

Jesus used the twelve disciples, none of whom had any training in the spreading of the Gospel, to reach an entire world and build a Church from scratch. These guys were fishermen and tax collectors who had normal everyday jobs, and God used them to reach thousands of people with the good news of the Gospel. Their impact is still felt today.

Will you be the one to lead people in your world to Jesus? You know the way if you know Jesus as your Saviour, so what stops you from leading others?

Dare to witness to those in your circle. You could be the link in the chain that pulls them to the One who can change them forever.

Day 41
Dare to Suffer

"I, JOHN, YOUR BROTHER AND PARTNER IN THE TRIBULATION AND THE KINGDOM AND THE PATIENT ENDURANCE THAT ARE IN JESUS, WAS ON THE ISLAND CALLED PATMOS ON ACCOUNT OF THE WORD OF GOD AND THE TESTIMONY OF JESUS."
REVELATION 1:9

In 95 AD, there was a Roman Emperor called Titus Flavius Domitanus. He was anti-Christian and persecuted the early Church with a passion. During one of his crusades he managed to capture the disciple, John. Instead of killing him, he decided to exile him to the island of Patmos. It was a harsh, remote island designed to kill and induce more suffering into the individuals there.

Domitanus wanted to break John's spirit. However, John was so full of the Holy Spirit that he couldn't be broken. Domitanus wanted to send John crazy however God allowed him to see the best vision of Heaven we have ever received.

I'm sure as John sat on that island by himself, he felt discouraged, alone, possibly even felt let down by God after all he had done for him. I am positive he suffered from the hot sun and lack of shade. The suffering that didn't make much sense to John has led to the entire Church of Jesus Christ having a hope of what comes after this life.

Maybe today, you are going through something that doesn't make much sense. Perhaps you feel discouraged and disheartened, or you are questioning why God allows you to go through this.

I want to encourage you to remember John. He died in exile. He died before the vision of Heaven was ever found. He died, not knowing his suffering would impact the Church. We may not see the impact of our suffering here on earth. God may never allow us to understand it before we get to Heaven; however, I am

83

confident that God uses everything we go through to expand His Kingdom, grow His Church, and develop our character.

We may not always like it, but God has a plan. We may never see it, but let's rest in the assurance that God is the same yesterday, today and forever, so His plan will never fail or be prevented. Let's encourage one another with this sure hope that if we suffer on account of living for Jesus, there is a plan and purpose within it. Jesus will never leave us on our own; through the suffering, let us keep our eyes on Him.

Dare to suffer. Jesus told us we would, and we can help enhance God's kingdom on earth if we dare to suffer for Christ.

Day 42
Dare to Create

"GO THEREFORE AND MAKE DISCIPLES OF ALL NATIONS, BAPTISING THEM IN THE NAME OF THE FATHER AND OF THE SON AND OF THE HOLY SPIRIT."
MATTHEW 28:19

Before Jesus went back to Heaven, He gave a few specific commandments that we were to do, with this one primarily being known as 'The Great Commission.' How mind blowing is it that our God, the God who could essentially do whatever He wanted in this world, gave this mission to mere human beings?

If God decided He wanted to, He could easily make Himself known to the whole of creation in an instant or allow all of creation to see His Glory for a moment the way He allowed Moses, but He doesn't. Instead, He will allow the whole of creation to choose Him for themselves, and how does He go about this incredible act of free will? By using us! You and me.

Despite all our faults and failings, despite God knowing everything about you and me, He still chooses to use us to bring about His great plan of Salvation. It excites me so much more to think that God chose me to help Him create disciples.

When we have a slow morning at home, we frequently do some baking. I can bake buns well on my own, and I can do them much better without little fingers poking into the bowl or little hands tipping half the flour down the side of the bowl. I can manage to make buns entirely on my own, but I decide not to because I love involving my children in the process. I love seeing them engaged in what I am doing, I love seeing them excited by the result, and I love seeing them enjoy the reward of their hard work.

Imagine how the Father's heart feels when He sees you and me engaged in His business. When He sees us proclaiming the good news to anyone we come into contact with. When He sees you and me telling someone about God's Salvation plan. Sure, He could do it himself, but as a parent myself, I begin to understand something of God's heart in wanting to involve us in the process.

Are you ready to go out and tell people the good news because our Father allows us to be involved in something He could do Himself? It is the most exciting opportunity you would ever be presented with!

So, are you willing to dare to go out and create disciples because of God's power at work within you? Imagine getting to Heaven and meeting someone there who heard you tell them of the good news. What an honour and reward that would be!

Day 43
Dare to be Unseen
"THE LORD SEES NOT AS MAN SEES; MAN LOOKS ON THE OUTWARD APPEARANCE, BUT THE LORD LOOKS ON THE HEART."
1 SAMUEL 16:7

One morning, I went out to the postbox and brought in a few letters. Upon opening them up, one of them contained a gift along with a note "For the Lennox family." That was all that the anonymous person said. It is such a kind gesture and a fantastic thing to remain unseen through it all.

To remain unseen is hard. You go without human praise, you go without human encouragement, and often you go without much recognition of what you are doing. I am not only talking about giving gifts anonymously, but also in deeds and work. Over the last few months, maybe more than ever, I have seen so many people working away in the background without wanting any recognition of what they are doing. They keep going, and they keep battling. They never give up and never want to be seen.

You could be a mother working away in your home, much of which goes unseen to the rest of the world. If they could only know how hard it is to get children to eat breakfast, never mind the rest of the day. And yet you continually teach them about God and build God's kingdom in your own home, unseen.

You may be a youth worker or a church pastor. So much work is in the background, yet all most people see is your sermon on a Sunday. They don't know how you sit with people in their homes at their worst moments. They don't see the hours of study in your own home as you try to wrap your head around Jesus' words. Yet you are building God's kingdom, unseen.

The unseen principle applies to so many people. Those slipping a gift in someone's letterbox, those who are teaching children in schools, health workers, police officers-so many people working away unseen but building God's kingdom.

So today, I want to encourage you, if that is you, God sees you. God sees your heart, God sees your motive, God sees your actions and God sees you. He will not let these actions of building His kingdom go unrewarded. He is such a good God and such a great Father, that He sees the littlest of deeds and will bless you for them. And how much greater is God's reward to us than man? How much greater is it to see God's kingdom being built than man's praise.

Dare to be unseen today, and you will receive your reward in Heaven, where it will never fade away!

Day 44
Dare to be Safe

"THE LORD IS MY SHEPHERD, I SHALL NOT WANT. HE MAKES ME LIE DOWN IN GREEN PASTURES." PSALM 23:1-2

I found something the other day. It was a birthday card. I came across it among some old letters that hadn't been touched in a while. It was the last card that I had received from mum. I was not expecting it, and it caught me off guard. And that pang of pain and grief came again. I didn't know how to process it. It almost hurts more when you're blindsided.

Sometimes in life, we expect ourselves to deal with grief, deal with pain, deal with shock and trauma on a timeline that means it's over and the door is closed. And when something threatens to open that door again, we want to shut it down and push it away. It feels threatening and painful, and we don't know how to deal with it.

That night I came to the prayer meeting at our church, and God showed me how.
Bring it to the shepherd.

In today's verse David is not encouraging us to lie down in laziness, but he reveals another trait in God's character to us. As a shepherd himself, David knew what he was talking about when he referred to God as a shepherd. He is telling us there is safety. If you know anything about sheep, you'll know they only lie down when they feel safe. There is safety with the shepherd.

Safety to bring your emotions to Him and process them correctly; to open up to Him about how you feel.
Safety to bring your grief, trauma, emotions, pain, hurt, and questions to Him and let Him show you the pathway through.
So I encourage you to bring your feelings, trauma, relationships, loss, and grief to the shepherd. It is a safe place to do it.

Some of us may benefit from having another person beside us as we do so, and that is healthy and responsible. Some of us may be comfortable going to the shepherd on our own. Either way, He is safe. He is the person to go to.

Go to the Shepherd, He is your safe place, and He will show you the path that is right for you. He will comfort you. And you shall not want with the shepherd beside you.

Dare to be safe with your Shepherd close at hand.

Day 45
Dare to shout

"ON THE SEVENTH DAY, YOU SHALL MARCH AROUND THE CITY SEVEN TIMES....THEN ALL THE PEOPLE SHALL SHOUT WITH A GREAT SHOUT, AND THE WALL OF THE CITY WILL FALL DOWN FLAT."
JOSHUA 6:4-5

Prayer is a vital part of our Christian life. I attend many prayer meetings in my work, and it is a pleasure. We get to sit and listen to people's hearts and burdens and see prayers answered frequently. Sometimes we speak to God in private, which is right and good. Jesus teaches us to do so. Often, some of the most significant battles that happen are battled in private, just between ourselves and God.

Through this story of Joshua and the walls of Jericho, I noticed that there is a time to be quiet and to shout. Some prayers must be quiet and private; other times, the battle is won in a shout raised from us to God in a public place.

God commanded Joshua to march around the walls of Jericho once a day for six days in silence. There is a time to be quiet. There is a time to listen to what God has to say. There is a time to wait on God. That is essential in our daily walk and in enabling us to move forward in our relationship with Him. This quiet and listening should be common daily practice in our lives.

Then, God told Joshua and the camp of Israel to shout on day seven, and the walls would come tumbling down, which happened. Sometimes we need to be quiet and sometime we ned to raise a shout in prayer - a shout in battle, a shout to other believers, a shout to God in a public prayer meeting for the fight to be won and the walls to fall around us. Sometimes we find ourselves marching around a battle for a lot longer than we should because we are not prepared to shout.

So I encourage you, next time you are in a prayer meeting with other believers, pray! Next time someone asks you what to pray for, speak up. Next time a battle seems to take a long time, a brutal battle you feel you shall never win, shout to God for help. There is a definite time to be quiet, but there is a definite time to raise a noise.

I encourage you to dare to shout and see what will change in your life because you dared to shout.

Day 46
Dare to Pray
"YOUR FATHER KNOWS WHAT YOU NEED BEFORE YOU ASK HIM"
MATTHEW 6:8

As a nurse, I was used to telling people what they had to do. I was used to telling students the daily rhythm of nursing life, explaining to patients how to change their health and sometimes challenging other health professionals about the best possible care. It is a trait I still often carry with me. I often go to the GP to tell them how to care for me or my children! Or I tell someone the best way I think they should approach a difficult challenge in their life. It is a trait I have learned can be useful and a hindrance.

I even noticed that I approach God that way on occasion. I pray to Him about a problem I am facing, and explain to Him how best to fix it! Please, tell me I am not on my own in this attitude?

How many times do we pray to God with an answer prepared about how He could best solve this issue? Yet, this verse tells us to approach God with a completely different attitude. Jesus, Himself, tells us that Our Father knows what we need before we even ask Him for it. How amazing is it, that Our Father continually watches us so closely, that He can tell what we are wanting.

I understand this to an extent. I know my daughters so well that frequently I can hand them something without them even asking me for it, I just know what they need. God knows us so intimately, so intently, and so knowledgeably that He already knows all that we need.

I am so thankful for a God who knows me that well. However, it also means that I need to approach prayer with a different attitude than trying to tell God the answer. It means I need to take a back seat in prayer, and leave the answering up to God because He knows already what the best outcome for me is. It means I need to be able to hand control over to God rather than keep it for myself. This is the difficulty that we face. If you have a personality like mine, that actually enjoys being able to help and fix problems, you may find this more of a challenge.

However, I am thankful that if God knows what I need already, then I can confidently hand control over to Him and leave the answer up to Him. It takes practice. Why not close this book and begin to bring your problem to God now, only in the attitude that you are laying it at His feet for His will to be done. The promise is that if we leave the answer up to God, we will have the best outcome for us. It may now always make sense, but we know we can trust Him because He is always good.

Dare to pray, and leave the answer to God, and see how much better it is than your own.

Day 47
Dare to be patient

"AND LET US NOT GROW WEARY OF DOING GOOD, FOR IN DUE SEASON WE WILL REAP, IF WE DO NOT GIVE UP."
GALATIANS 6:9

They sat on our window sill for about a week until I was about to throw them in the bin. We had been given watercress seeds as an activity for Sunday School in a lesson of how when you plant, you reap. However, I was still waiting to see if there was anything to reap. A week of looking at tiny seeds that didn't seem to change over the course of the week had led me to put them in the bin out of my way. As I lifted the egg trough to dump the lot, I took another look and saw tiny white sprouts coming out of the seeds. It was enough to make me place them back on the windowsill and watch, and within another week we had a crop of watercress sitting in our kitchen.

Sometimes in our spiritual life, we have been praying and asking God for a change in our life or circumstances and we think nothing is happening because we do not see a turnaround in what we are facing. We have a timeline which we hope God will work in, and when He does not we are tempted to quit. We are so used to immediate results in the world we live in, that it has caused us to have no patience for anything in our life, including God's work.

However, God does not work to our timeline or conditions. When we give our lives over to Him, we are declaring that we will act according to His will, wait according to His timing and have patience so that we will see a harvest in our lives.

God can see our life in a different way than we can. God sees the end from the beginning, (Isaiah 46:10) His path for us is far higher than our own as are His thoughts toward us, (Isaiah 55:9). Therefore, we can fully trust in God's timings for our lives, even if they seem slower than we would like, because we can trust that He knows what is best for us.

If I had thrown the watercress in the bin because I was too impatient, I would have missed the harvest that finally came to us. In the same way, should we quit our spiritual walk because we feel the timing is too slow, we could miss a substantial harvest that God has promised us if we are patient.

Dare to be patient as we wait on God to move. The result is His work and He has promised it will be worth it if we wait.

Day 48
Dare to follow

"TRUST IN THE LORD WITH ALL YOUR HEART, AND DO NOT LEAN ON YOUR OWN UNDERSTANDING. IN ALL YOUR WAYS, ACKNOWLEDGE HIM, AND HE SHALL MAKE STRAIGHT YOUR PATHS."
PROVERBS 3:5-6

When my mum and dad got engaged, my Grandparents gave them this verse on a card, and it became their life verse ever since. Ever since they started life together, they believed God knew the best path for their life and how God would lead them and take care of them. They believed if they laid down everything before God, they would have direction in what to do. It was not always an easy pathway, it was not always a fun pathway, but it provided them with the best path for their lives. They often told us so, and we often saw it for ourselves.

Emily is now 19 months old and can walk by herself. She enjoys going out for walks with me while Hannah is at school and loves it when I do not take the buggy but allow her to walk independently. However, Emily still does not fully grasp the concept of going where I am going because it is the safest path for her. She still does not realise that out the back of our house there are many large rocks that can trip her up, which I can see and steer her around. She will often run straight on without me and trip and land in a heap.

I do not try to steer her path because I do not want her to get to the play park across those rocks. I show her the best way to prevent her from getting hurt, from tripping over things that can harm her, or from ending up having to go home early because she is lying in a heap.

God wants to direct our paths, not to stop us from getting the best possible life, but so that he can show us where the pitfalls lie before we get hurt. Eventually, as we continue in the Christian life, we understand that His path for us is safer than

97

our path for ourselves. So we can start to gain ground against the enemy because we are walking straight and upright, instead of walking around hurt from things we have faced in our life.

God wants to direct our pathway. When Emily follows me rather than herself, we end up at the destination where we intend to go. We have a great time, and she finds herself living her best life because she followed the one who knew the right path to go. So, when we follow God, we will find that we have life in all its fullness, because we followed the One who knew the right path for us.

So I encourage you today, maybe for the first time, to start to follow God instead of your path. That may mean creating a relationship with Him for the first time, giving Him your life, and declaring that you will follow Him. Not so that He can have power over you, but so that together you will gain ground in this life and the next. If you follow Him already, give Him everything. Start to read your Bible and listen to Him. He will not steer you wrong if you fully trust Him and let Him direct your paths.

If you dare to follow, you will find the way to life in all its fullness!

Day 49
Dare to forgive

"AND FORGIVE US OUR DEBTS, AS WE ALSO HAVE FORGIVEN OUR DEBTORS."
MATTHEW 6:12

If you have more than one child, you will understand the current struggle in our house of teaching our girls how to forgive each other. When they pull each other's hair, steal toys, snatch from the other, or wreck a carefully formulated game, forgiveness is required. No matter how old we are, it does not come naturally to forgive someone who has wronged us.

Forgiveness is constantly required in life but not easy to learn. It is hard when someone continually hurts you. I am not referring to a game of make-believe, but to more complex situations in your life. Maybe you have been hurt by someone who broke a promise, broke a marriage vow, broke your trust, broke your heart. So many situations in our world can lead to unforgiveness forming in our lives.

Unforgiveness can be so dangerous. It can lead to bitterness in our lives, leading to grudges being held and family breakdowns. More seriously, it can lead to a breakdown in communication between God and us. He has frequently told us that we need to forgive others as He forgives us to experience a close relationship with Him.

I do not pretend to understand your situation or your pain. I do not pretend to realise all the hurt you have experienced in your life, and I am not saying that it does not matter. I am not telling you that broken promises, broken trust, hurt, or pain is null and void. It is genuine and takes a lot of work to recover from.

However, I heard it once said that forgiving someone is not forgetting what they did, but handing their judgement over to God to deal with instead of you. It means you can remember

99

what happened it without the sting of pain that comes with it. Forgiveness of that kind comes directly from God alone, and He alone can give us the supernatural grace that is required to forgive someone who has hurt us. Who better to provide us with the grace to forgive than the one who forgave the very people who hung him on the cross.

So, it may not happen today, and it may not lead to complete forgiveness for a while; some of us may need someone else to help us make this journey and that is a responsible action. But forgiveness starts with a conversation with God, telling Him of our desire to forgive and asking for His grace to start this journey. Forgiveness is the key to a full and free life from bitterness. Begin to forgive, begin to have that conversation with God, and search for that grace to let past hurts go.

The difference in life and your relationship with God as you begin to let hurts go will amaze you as you dare to forgive.

Day 50
Dare to leave

**"AND PETER ANSWERED HIM, "LORD, IF IT IS YOU, COMMAND ME TO COME TO YOU ON THE WATER." HE SAID, "COME." SO PETER GOT OUT OF THE BOAT AND WALKED ON THE WATER, AND CAME TO JESUS. BUT WHEN HE SAW THE WIND, HE WAS AFRAID, AND BEGINNING TO SINK, HE CRIED OUT, "LORD, SAVE ME."
MATTHEW 14:28-30**

Peter. One of Jesus' twelve disciples. One of His closest friends. He had followed Him, and he had seen miracles performed by Him. He had seen people changed by Him. Now when they are caught in the storm in the middle of the sea, being tossed by the wind and the waves, He sees Him again. Can you imagine? For a fisherman, a storm was not uncommon to be caught in, but something about this storm was different. In the splash of the sea on their faces, the wind making their eyes water, and the howling gales all around, they see a figure walking toward them, not only walking, but He starts calling them out to walk with Him.

So many times, poor Peter gets a bad rap for this moment in history. He is publicly humiliated when a moment of fantastic faith turns into a scene of doubt and fear. When he takes his eyes off Jesus, he begins to sink under the waves. He begins to fall into the 'what ifs' and the sea of uncertainty. And suddenly, his moment of faith is forgotten by so many. People talk of how he doubted instead of how he jumped. People discuss how he needed to be rescued instead of taking Jesus at His word.

This happens so frequently in the Church of Jesus across the world. People see someone's failures instead of someone's faith. They see their doubt instead of their decisions being made to get them there. And so often, a person's journey is forgotten in the middle of a moment of failure.

Peter jumped out of the boat at Jesus' word. Yes, he sank when he took his eyes off Jesus, but the point we need to remember is that eleven others were still on the boat when Peter needed to be rescued. Eleven people were also called but did not move. Eleven people could also practice their faith but decided not to. Eleven people were driven by doubt before they even took a step, rather than doubt in the middle of their faith journey.

Even though Peter needed to be rescued, he took a step of faith in the first place, and that is what we need to see. He ended up with a story to tell about how he got out of the boat and walked on water, even though it did not go quite to plan. He had a story to tell about how he felt Jesus lifting him out of the storm and how it proved God never lets us drown in our doubt and uncertainty. Maybe today, you are the one needing to be rescued. Perhaps you took a step of faith and got tossed by doubt, and now you feel like a failure. Be encouraged; you have started on a journey, like many before you. Be inspired that Peter became the rock of the Church. Be encouraged that Jesus specialises in rescue missions that start people off again. Be encouraged that you have a story to tell that others who never took a step have not.

Dare to leave the boat, hear the call, know that the call is intended for you, and get out of the ship. See where your steps of faith will take you when you hear the call, and keep your eyes on the One who can make you walk on the storm.

Day 51
Dare to Begin

"DO NOT DESPISE THESE SMALL BEGINNINGS, FOR THE LORD REJOICES TO SEE THE WORK BEGIN."
ZECHARIAH 4:10A (NEW LIVING TRANSLATION)

"Mummy, can you help me..." is a frequently asked question in our house. This morning we were playing, and Hannah said, "Mummy can you help me build a bridge with these cushions?"
"Yes," I replied and got down on the floor, ready to begin the bridge-building.
"Mummy, can you help me build a bridge?" Hannah asked again.
"Yes, I'm here waiting," I said.
"Mummy, can you help me build a bridge?" a third time.
"Hannah, I'm here waiting... Start building, and I'll help you." I said it again.
"Hannah, I'm here waiting... Start building, and I'll help you." I said it again.
And finally, the bridge-building started when she eventually realised I was waiting for her to make the first move before I stepped in to help. Hannah and I built the bridge together because she stopped asking me for help and started working.

Many times in our Christian life, we are the same. God gives us a vision, a plan for the future, so we stop and pray, as we absolutely should, and ask for help. We may stop to pray again and ask for help. Sometimes we pray again and ask for help.

We may never actually start because we wait for help to come first before we make a move. And all the while, God is waiting to help, to offer us power, to give us supernatural strength, and yet we keep asking.

Don't get me wrong, there is a place for waiting on God, a time for prayer for help, a reason why we pray and often fast before starting a new venture. There is a time and place to ask.

There is then a moment when we have to trust that we will receive the help we have prayed for. Peter had to move his feet out of the boat to see if he could walk on water through Jesus' power. Paul had to set sail and visit new places to see the Holy Spirit change lives. Moses had to start to walk through the Red Sea to watch the waters part.

Some of you today need to begin. You have asked and sought long enough. You have sat waiting for an answer for a while. You know what God wants, understand the vision, and have been imparted the plan. Now it's your time to begin the work. If it is from God, help will follow with the first step of obedience. Hannah could have asked for help all morning. I was willing and waiting to offer it, but she had to begin to complete it. So do you!

Don't keep waiting. Dare to begin and see the power God will divulge upon you.

Day 52
Dare to know your worth

"ARE NOT FIVE SPARROWS SOLD FOR TWO PENNIES? AND NOT ONE OF THEM IS FORGOTTEN BEFORE GOD. WHY EVEN THE HAIRS OF YOUR HEAD ARE ALL NUMBERED. FEAR NOT; YOU ARE OF MORE VALUE THAN MANY SPARROWS."
LUKE 12:6-7

Jesus spoke these words. While He lived here on earth, He did not just want to tell us about Heaven and Hell. Jesus did not just want to let us know about our sin and His miracles. He took the time to tell us how much value is placed on us by God. How amazing that God values us. The Bible states this frequently, more than 100 times, telling us how valuable we are to God.

The Bible tells us: God rejoices over us with singing (Zephaniah 3:17); we are not a mistake but are purposely formed by the Lord from inside the womb (Jeremiah 1:5); we are His workmanship made for a reason (Ephesians 2:10); we are chosen (1 Peter 2:9); God loves to hear our voice (SoS 2:14), and God will never forget us (Isaiah 49:15).

We are valued, and because we are loved, Jesus said that we should not fear. We should not worry because God thinks of us. We should not fear because God knows us. We should not fear because God cares for us. We should not fear because God knows what we need. We should not worry because God values you despite your circumstances or what you have been told in your life. No matter what you have done, where you have been, how you have lived or what your background is, God values you.

Maybe today you need to remember this fact. Perhaps you need to quote it over to yourself again. Perhaps you need to tell someone in your world about this. And begin to live like you are highly valued by the King of Kings. Lift your head, straighten those shoulders and live in the truth that God cares about you.

The Devil hates it; he will do everything to make you forget it because he knows it is true. He knows the power that is in it. So remind yourself and others frequently. You are valued.

Dare to know your worth in Christ.

Day 53
Dare to be Grateful

"THIS IS THE DAY THAT THE LORD HAS MADE; LET US REJOICE AND BE GLAD IN IT."
PSALM 118:24

Do you ever have one of those moments where God pulls you up on something, and it just makes you cringe because you realise He is right even though 10 seconds ago you felt justified in your feelings? That happens to me frequently in my walk with God!

On one such occasion, I was having the type of day where nothing seemed to go right. Hannah was sick on me in the morning and at night, I kept losing everything, the dog was in my way, we got an email that was frustrating and required effort to sort, and I just didn't feel well. About 5pm, I was frustratingly walking through the kitchen when I exclaimed, ``Everything is just rubbish!"

And I heard Him. I listened to His small voice reply, "Is it though? You've just left your warm living room with a fire blazing to go and check on your 3rd meal of the day cooking, your daughter is playing happily, and your husband is away earning more money to live on. Your home is standing, you have breath in your lungs, and a baby is growing healthy within you. Is it all rubbish?"

Sometimes in life, we focus on what is going wrong, and we miss the many blessings from God to us. It's ok to feel frustrated at times, and it's ok to feel like a day has been challenging, but sometimes, and rightly so, I think God likes to remind us gently that all isn't as bad as we think. I believe God loves when we thank Him even at the end of a tough day, because we know He has been good to us even though things look chaotic or complex.

May we never forget how good God has been to us in this life. How thankful we should be with His many blessings to us daily. Maybe for some of us it is only that we have air in our lungs, but we should still be thankful. We can always be thankful for the greatest blessing He has given to us of His one and only Son. His Son who left Heaven and came to this world to die, purely because He loves us. The God who gave all that He had to us to help us see how much He cares for us.

Let us take today's verse as an anthem we try to live by. This day that God has made, we will be glad and rejoice because of the abundance of blessings God has provided for us. Let us be an example to a world driven by a 'me' mentality, of how you can be thankful for the seemingly small gifts God gives to us. Of course there will be times this is difficult, but if the overall anthem of our life is gratefulness, we will find it easier to stay thankful in the harder times.

So today, or tonight, before you sleep, try and count three blessings from today and be thankful. They may seem small, but I guarantee it will lift your eyes from your problems to what you can dare to be grateful for, and that alone is a successful end to a day!

Day 54
Dare to Hold Fast

"ALL YOUR CHILDREN SHALL BE TAUGHT BY THE LORD, AND GREAT SHALL BE THE PEACE OF YOUR CHILDREN."
ISAIAH 54:13

There is a picture of this verse that hangs in our hallway. It is the promise I was given by God when I was pregnant with Hannah, probably about this time three years ago. It jumped off the page to me one day, and I have prayed it over our girls ever since as a promise from God for their lives.

There was a time when I became more anxious for our girl's safety, health and protection. I had this verse hanging in our hall as a reminder that God had promised He would always be in control, but over the everyday business, I had forgotten it. On a day I was particularly anxious for them, my eyes rested on this verse again. I remembered the promise from God. I remembered that He gave this to me specifically for our family. And I suddenly felt a shift.

Nothing had changed in our circumstances. Nothing had changed on the news, Covid-19 was still going strong. Nothing had changed in our family, we had two vulnerable children. Yet something changed- my perspective, my hope and my focus. They shifted from it all resting on me and what I should do to God and His promise over our lives.

That's why it is so important to hold fast to God's promises. To stand firm on what God promised to you in years gone by, to remember what He said to you before your circumstances changed, or just to know that He is still God and can handle all of this. I know it can be hard to keep faith when it seems like such a long time between a promise and a circumstance changing. However, we see it time and again in the Bible. Abraham waited twenty five years, Noah waited seventy five years and Joseph waited thirteen years. If you are waiting on a promise coming to pass, you are not on your own!

You have good company, and good examples of seeing that circumstances do not determine your outcome.

What do you need to remember tonight? Before you sleep, switch off the news and all the circumstances around you. And focus on what God once told you and dare to hold fast to that Word. Write them out so you can see them clearly every day. Speak them aloud so you can hear them. Repeat them aloud when the devil comes to try and steal your peace. Declare them over your family, believing that God will be faithful and will enable your promises to come to pass.

Dare to hold fast. What's your promise? Why not write it down here!

Day 55
Dare to Wake Up
"BESIDES THIS, YOU KNOW THE TIME, THAT THE HOUR HAS COME FOR YOU TO WAKE FROM SLEEP. FOR SALVATION IS NEARER TO US NOW THAN WHEN WE FIRST BELIEVED"
ROMANS 13:11

I do not like to be woken out of my sleep. I was always a good sleeper until I had children. Now, if I get four hours of uninterrupted sleep, I wonder if my children are ok! If you are a parent, you will know the small churn in your stomach when you wake to your child shouting for you, and you know you have to rise to help them. There is part of you that would prefer to sleep, but you will get up for your child because they need you.

Sleeping Christianity is not what the Bible teaches! In fact, it is the opposite, get up and go! Wake up, get dressed and get to work!

Why? Because there is a lost world out there that needs you! There are people who God loves who He needs you to reach! Some Christians are happy to sit around and let other people do the work while relaxing.

Rev 3:1-6 talks about the church of Sardis, in modern-day Turkey, more commonly known as the sleeping church. This church appeared to be a living church, a Christian church. It was packed and lively and seemed to be thriving, but spiritually it was dying and sleeping. A command is given within the letter to this church: "Wake up and strengthen what remains and is about to die" (Rev 3:1).

Throughout the Bible, we see the danger of spiritual sleep. The virgins in Matthew 25:6 were sleeping and weren't ready for the bridegroom to come for them. Nearly worse than that, the ones who were willing and prepared let the others sleep rather than shake them awake and tell them what could happen. Jonah fell asleep and didn't even realise the threat was around him (Jonah 1:5).

However, Paul here will not let that happen to the church in Rome, and the Angel of the church of Sardis wasn't going to let it happen. They made a shout, and they made some noise to wake the sleeping Christians. You want to harness God's power in your life, you want victory in your life, you want to see God be the God of the Bible in your life, then you have to wake up!

Maybe you have been sleeping in your spiritual life. Enough is enough. It's time to wake up. I am convinced we are closer to the end times, and the Church needs to make some noise to rescue those who are deaf to the good news and those who are blind. We need to wake those who have gone to sleep and begin a movement of the Church of Jesus Christ that will impact this world.

Dare to wake up! The world is waiting on you.

Day 56
Dare to Get Dressed

"THE NIGHT IS FAR GONE; THE DAY IS AT HAND. SO THEN, LET US CAST OFF THE WORKS OF DARKNESS AND PUT ON THE ARMOUR OF LIGHT. "
ROMANS 13:12

So you're finally awake and starting to feel things and see things again. It may only be a wee bit, but you're getting there! Ask God to begin turning that tiny spark into a flame. But one thing that needs to be done is we need to change.

When you wake, you need to start taking off your PJs and putting on suitable clothes for the day you are going to face. We are told in 1 Peter 5:18 that the Devil prowls around us like a roaring lion seeking whom he may devour. We are vulnerable and weak compared to the Devil's powers. We are no match for him on our own. In our spiritual rags, we are his prey, and he is ready to take us.

But God is a good God, and He gives us the appropriate clothing for such a fight. It says in this passage to put on the "armour of light". Armour isn't the most comfortable item of clothing to wear, but it is necessary. We can try to live the Christian life in comfort instead of practical, but the lion is always here, waiting for whom he may devour. Get up and put your armour on!

Ephesians 6:10-20 tells us about that armour. It is complete, and it is full!

Helmet of salvation
Breastplate of righteousness
Belt of truth
Sword of Spirit
Shield of faith
Shoes of peace.

Completely covered to enter into the day that God has set for us! Put this on every day, and you will be able to stand against any attack from the enemy. When He starts putting those old thoughts back in your head, use your helmet. Realise your mind and head are protected, and say that to the enemy. Fill your mind with the Bible, with words of truth. When you start to doubt whether you can do it, fasten your belt and realise what the truth is in that situation. When you feel a temptation coming against you, use your sword and speak the words of Jesus while you fight. Use your armour and start being in warrior combat mode.

Dare to get dressed to make a difference in this world in this day and age. The world needs a Church who is awake and suitably dressed, so we can, in Jesus Name and strength, win the war against the powers of darkness with the armour of light as our defence.

Day 57
Dare to Get Moving

"LET US WALK PROPERLY AS IN THE DAYTIME, NOT IN ORGIES AND DRUNKENNESS, NOT IN SEXUAL IMMORALITY AND SENSUALITY, NOT IN QUARRELLING AND JEALOUSY."
ROMANS 13:13

I remember being taught as a student nurse what was expected of us during our training. There were high expectations of a nurse. You were not allowed to get drunk in public, and you could not have a criminal record. You were not allowed to become loud and disorderly. To be a nurse, you were expected to live a particular lifestyle, conduct yourself in a certain way, display certain mannerisms to allow people to put their confidence in you within the hospital setting. Of course, not everyone held these standards as firmly as they were put across, but they were made clear that this was what was expected of us. It was not to spoil our fun but to live in a way that displayed the gravity of the occupation we were to embark on. There would be people depending on us who needed to know they could trust us.

As Christians, we are expected to live a certain way, carry certain mannerisms, live in a particular lifestyle that makes it obvious who we follow. The Bible says we should "walk properly as in the daytime" (Romans 13:13). This verse refers to Jesus' words in John 3:19, "people loved the darkness rather than the light because their works were evil."

We are to be different from the people in this world, not because we are better than them but because we have been changed from the inside out, and this should be obvious in how we walk and conduct ourselves.

Do you dare to get moving in the way that Jesus encouraged us to? Dare to get moving with love, joy, peace, gentleness, goodness, meekness, self-control, faithfulness and patience. We need to dare to begin to mirror Jesus to people who do not know Him properly.

If we have specific ways to conduct ourselves in earthly occupations, what makes us think that we as citizens of Heaven should not acknowledge the way to walk while we are here on earth? Could it be that Jesus knew if people saw these qualities within us, they may just be drawn to the Father a lot faster?

May we never be a stumbling block to anyone, but encourage people to look at the Father through how we dare to move here on earth.

Day 58
Dare to Deny Yourself
"BUT PUT ON THE LORD JESUS CHRIST, AND MAKE NO PROVISION FOR THE FLESH, TO GRATIFY ITS DESIRES."
ROMANS 13:14

We don't only need to put on the armour, but we must take off the works of darkness for the armour to stick. We must take off all the old ways of living and become a new creation. We can't wear both, it doesn't work. You can't expect to get victory in your life when you are still standing with one foot in the Devil's kingdom. So not only do we have to wake up, but we have to fully get rid of the old life that put us to sleep in the first place and walk into the new.

I was interested to know what all these things have in common, why this list of things, as opposed to all the other sins that he could have listed. I came up with the answer, this group, in particular, is all about me! Immoral behaviour, getting drunk, having sex, wanting everything for yourself, it's all about me! Full of pride.

This life is not primarily for me to enjoy myself. But my life is about becoming more like Jesus. That is what the Bible teaches, from start to finish; it is all about the plan of Salvation first and then about becoming more like Christ. And how do I do it? Let Him chip away at me and get rid of these things that I know are not right. Let him dig deep and get the pride out of me. Let Him make me His masterpiece.

And how does this happen? How do I make sure I am becoming more like Him? Today's verse says "make no provision for the flesh." That doesn't mean physical provision for your body, but spiritually. It could mean getting a block on your internet or throwing away books you know have unhelpful content. It could mean clearing your cupboards of food or drink, that is constantly getting the better of you. It could mean getting out of bed half an hour earlier to do your quiet time. Make no provision. Not some, not a wee bit-none!

And what happens when something doesn't get the provision it needs-it dies! If you were to go without food long enough in your life, you would die. Don't make provision for the flesh anymore, don't purposely go out of your way to create space in your life for things that aren't helpful! Get rid of them! There is a bigger picture than you in this world, and there is more significant work to be done than looking after yourself here! Start moving, start going after it! Stop wasting time on things that don't matter, move on!

Put on Jesus Christ. He is good, kind, gracious, and we are also to be all those things, so when people look at us, they see Him in us! But Jesus is also fierce, and He is majestic. He has power. Jesus is mighty, passionate and strong! We are not just to be gentle, meek and mild; we are to be fierce, to go against the enemies attack with the power of Jesus Christ within us. We are to come against the Devil's plans for our lives and counteract it by putting Jesus on as spiritual clothing!

Dare to deny yourself to allow Jesus access to everything in your life.

Day 59
Dare to Build

"NOAH WAS A RIGHTEOUS MAN, BLAMELESS IN HIS GENERATION. NOAH WALKED WITH GOD.."
GENESIS 6:9

I am sitting on my bed writing this as I wait for my children to finally fall asleep. If you are a parent, you will know the anticipation with this part of the day! I have just come in from settling our eldest in bed, having read to her Noah and the Ark. It is a well-known story. God tells the only godly man in the world that He will send a flood to cleanse the earth from all the ungodly and wicked people of that time, and begin again. However, He wants to save Noah and his family, so he tells them to build an ark with room for whoever else wants to join them and trust God. The flood comes, and the world is cleansed, and God sends a rainbow as a sign that He will never again flood the earth.

The part I don't think has struck me before is how long it was between God telling Noah to build an ark and the flood appearing. In my mind, it was maybe a year. According to 'Answers in Genesis', it took 55-75 years. Once Noah built the boat, all the animals and the people went inside, and the door was closed. It was another seven days before the rain came.

Can you imagine the period between God telling Noah to build an ark and the rain beginning? Can you imagine the questions Noah would have had! As people laughed and scorned him, as his family questioned him, as his hands were raw with building and his mind filled with the task at hand. Through every sleepless night he had and every dinner that had gone cold by the time he made it home. I am sure there were many, many times he doubted. I'm sure he often wondered if he had started something that he could not finish. I often wonder if he sat looking at this construction, wondering if God had made a mistake or if he had heard God wrong. I am sure as he sat in the ark waiting in the rain, hearing the world outside, doubts and fears crept in again.

Maybe God has told you to do something. To go a particular path or begin a specific ministry. Maybe God has told you to start something that seems strange to everyone else around you. Maybe people have been planting doubts in your mind, telling you it has gone too long without fruit or any evidence of what God had said would happen, and you are starting to feel like giving up.

Noah, I am sure, felt like this until he heard the first drop of rain on the roof. Then God's plan, all that God had told him, all that God had promised and warned of, came to be for all to see. Keep building in your world. Keep following the plan God has shown you. You may feel like worries or doubts are becoming more robust than the promise. Tell someone, write it down for all to see. Others may not get it. Others may not understand.

If you have a clear vision, a clear path, and a clear word from God, dare to build what God has placed in front of you. You will see God's word come to pass before your very eyes.

Day 60
Dare to be Dependent

"BEHOLD GOD IS MY HELPER; THE LORD IS THE UPHOLDER OF MY LIFE."
PSALM 54:4

"Mummy, I will do it," is a frequent statement in our home.

Both our children are becoming much more independent and need to do things for themselves. Emily loves to do up the side belt buckle herself, and if you try and do it for her, a tantrum will quickly follow. Hannah loves to help Emily do things and takes her big sister role very seriously. She helps Emily get down the big step at our front door, helps her walk if the path is unsteady, and helps her brush her hair before we go out. However, sometimes a power struggle ensues between Hannah wanting to help and Emily wanting to be independent.

A natural part of growing up is that we want to be more independent. However, if we read the Bible correctly, the opposite is true in our spiritual lives. We should not be getting more independent. We should, in fact, realise that we need more and more of God rather than of ourselves.

God does not ever expect us to do anything for ourselves spiritually. We have responsibilities. We are to pray and listen, witness, and help others, which are expected of us as we grow spiritually. We are never expected to become independent because that is impossible. Jesus ensures that throughout the Bible, it is clearly stated we are to ask for help from our Father God and not tackle life on our own. The more we grow spiritually, the more we read the Bible, the more we become like Jesus, we should see that we can never move forward without His help in our lives.

We begin to see how much we need to ask Him for help, support, direction, understanding, wisdom and knowledge. So, if you have been trying to do things for yourself or clean your life

121

up, understand the path ahead or walk in your strength. Take a wee spiritual health check and see where your dependence lies. If you think it lies more in yourself than in God, talk to Him, admit where you are, and ask God to help you depend on Him. Physical independence is a sign of growth and healthy development. Spiritual dependence is a sign of spiritual maturity.

You do not have to do this yourself; help is there if you learn to ask and dare to depend on God.

Day 61
Dare to Ask
"HE WAS A MIGHTY MAN OF VALOUR, BUT HE WAS A LEPER."
2 KINGS 5:1

How often do we look at someone we see on social media, in the street, at our church and think they must have a perfect life? How many times do we try to make out that all in our life is going smoothly when, deep down, we know that there are problems undermining the image that we are putting out to the public?

Naaman was the sort of guy who appeared to have it all on the outside looking in. The start of the verse speaks of how he is a commander, he is great with his boss, and he is favoured. It speaks of how the Lord gave him victory against his enemies, and how he is a mighty man with great courage. What a guy! What a life he must have lived and how everyone must have envied him. The verse finished with a sad phrase that turns this upside down, 'he was a leper.'

This illness of leprosy disgraced people in Biblical times, which caused isolation, the disease that brought death and discrimination to families. Naaman was a leper. He had two choices, in my opinion. He could ask for help, or he could hide his illness. He was commander of the army, and he was in high favour. He was great with his boss- he had a lot to lose should this become public knowledge. He could have been cast aside from all he had and forced to be exiled from the community entirely until death came. Hiding probably seemed like quite a good idea. Hiding what was wrong, covering up the patches that were appearing and making out all was well so life could try and keep going.

So often in our lives, when we have something that brings shame or hurt or pain to a situation or a family circumstance or just to our reputation, we try to hide it. We try to cover it up or pretend it is not there. We do not like to admit that the problem exists. So mental illness is on the rise because so many people are trying to wear a mask that everything is ok when it is not.

The good news in this story is that Naaman asked for help. He did not just ask; he went and sought it out. He went out of his way to speak with the King, travelled a great distance and washed in a dirty river to get help. He even went as far as to listen to a servant girl to make sure that his disease was cured. And God healed him because he asked and listened to the correct person.

If you have a circumstance bringing you shame, a problem that you do not know how to deal with, or an issue that could lead to you being isolated, ask for help. Be specific. You don't have to announce that you need help or hint that you need assistance, or brag that you need help. Simply ask. Go to someone wiser than you who knows where you can go for the service you require. Most of all, go to God and admit the problem before Him and ask for wisdom- If any of you lacks wisdom, let him ask God who gives (wisdom) generously to all.' James 1:5. Do not hide your problems and hope they go away. Isolation, secrecy or pretence is not the way forward.

Dare to ask people who genuinely care for you, and a God who loves you, for what you need. It makes facing hard times so much easier when you have people beside you.

Day 62
Dare to Listen

"GO AND WASH IN THE JORDAN SEVEN TIMES, AND YOUR FLESH SHALL BE RESTORED."
2 KINGS 5:10

We have two responsibilities when we come to God with a problem in our lives. We are to ask and to listen. Listening is hard in this noisy culture full of busyness at every turn. Many of us cannot sit on the sofa quietly anymore. The TV must be on in the background, or we must flick through social media before settling. As I am writing this, I currently have a children's TV show and an 18-month-old yelling at a toy that is not working correctly. It is hard to find peace to listen to God properly.

So we have to be intentional. I have discovered listening to God properly involves carving time out of your day. It is tough to hear God as we go about our normal daily activities. We see in the Bible that sometimes He interrupted daily activities to speak to people, such as Mary, the mother of Jesus, or when he called the apostles. However, sometimes He also speaks in a whisper, such as with Elijah outside the cave.

Our family has begun to take time out of our weak to go somewhere quiet and listen. We sometimes read, listen to a talk, worship music, or sit quietly. Often I find God talks to me most as I walk; Jonny finds he hears most as he sits. Find what way works best for you to listen, and then pay attention.

Naaman had come and asked for help. Now it was his responsibility to listen to the answer. For us to hear God's answer, we must be part of God's family. Maybe you have never heard the answer because you are not part of this family yet. Today could be your day to begin a relationship with Him. The Bible says, "My sheep hear my voice, and I know them, and they follow me." (John 10:27). If you know God, understand that He has heard your cry and will answer you. As we find out tomorrow, he may answer you with something you do not always appreciate. However, He will always answer.

We will be able to take steps with complete confidence that the God of Heaven has commanded our path because we dared to listen.

Day 63
Dare to Obey

"SO HE WENT DOWN AND DIPPED HIMSELF SEVEN TIMES IN THE JORDAN...AND HIS FLESH WAS RESTORED LIKE THE FLESH OF A LITTLE CHILD."
2 KINGS 5:14

There was a choice here to be made. I'm not too fond of choices. I prefer someone to tell me something to do and leave me with no other option but to do it. Naaman had asked, and he had listened to the solution. Now he had a choice. He could either obey or turn away. He could either humble himself or allow pride to control him.

Naaman had listened, but he did not like what he heard. Could you imagine going back to the King when he had let you and your servants travel 450km to have dramatic healing from the prophet, to return and tell him that you just had to dip in a dirty river seven times for recovery! He did not like being told that the option was simple. We sometimes like drama and a good story to tell people what has happened to us. Occasionally we don't appreciate a simple solution to a challenging situation. Naaman did not like this simple solution of washing.

Naaman had listened, but he did not like having to humble himself. He was the captain of the army. He was a great friend of the King. Who was this prophet who thought that he should bathe in an ordinary dirty river? We sometimes prefer our healing to be clean-cut and easy. We may not like it when it causes mess and hardship. We often hope that God will take our messy situation away without much effort from us; we think that God should be able to remove everything from our pathway without having to involve any obedience on our part.

Thankfully Naaman had people around him to encourage him to obey, even a confusing command. God knew what He was doing when He gave us the Church to be around us as

Christians. People to guide us, advise us, and rebuke us when we need it. People who care for us and help us to see past the confusion into what God wants to show us.

So today, if you are at a crossroad where God is challenging you to obey, and you don't fully understand, approach someone you trust with wisdom and ask them for an objective view on the situation. If you need healing in your life, listen to what God says and obey it. God's way can sometimes be more complex than we would like, messier than we would like, or require more humility than we would like. However, Naaman experienced complete healing when he went God's way instead of his own. Could it be that your healing, solution, or security are only a step of obedience away?

Listen to what God says and dare to obey it. You can experience freedom because you went God's way!

Day 64
Dare to be Loved
"FOR GOD SO LOVED THE WORLD, THAT HE GAVE HIS ONLY SON, THAT WHOEVER BELIEVES IN HIM SHOULD NOT PERISH BUT HAVE ETERNAL LIFE."
JOHN 3:16

I do not know if you are a St. Valentine's Day enthusiast. Over the years it has become more commercialised than ever. The shop across the road from us has taken up half of the doorway with chocolates, flowers, balloons and teddy bears, all for people to give to the one they love as a demonstration of their feelings for each other.

The real story behind St. Valentine is a completely different tale from the roses and chocolates we think of today. Valentine was a Roman Priest in 270 AD who was persecuted and martyred because He stood up for what He believed in. He stood up for his conviction and as such was put to death. Before his death he prayed for healing for a blind lady named Julia, when she received her sight he had left her a note signed, 'your valentine', thus where we get the idea of sending cards to show love to one another.

St. Valentine's Day may be held in regard to love and showing others love. However, Jesus set the standard for real true love. He showed us what love actually looks like rather than just feels like. Jesus personified love when He came to this earth, He acted it out before people's very eyes. Real love, the Bible tells us, is "that someone lay down his life for His friends." (John 15:13)

Jesus did this very act for us when He died on the cross. He laid down His life in exchange for ours, took beatings so that we could walk free, died so that we could live, was separated from God so we could be united. Sin had caused a division from God in Genesis 2, in the Garden of Eden. God made man to have communion with Him, and when Adam and Eve ate the forbidden fruit, that communion and relationship with God was broken.

However, the Good News was provided for us as soon as the relationship was destroyed. God promised a Saviour who would give us access to God again, renew the relationship, and allow us to start over, because He would take the price of sin upon himself so we would not have to. The price of sin is death, and so God the Father and God the Son devised a plan where God the Son would accept this penalty so we could live forever. Amazing news- the Gospel of Jesus! God the Father gave His only Son to take our penalty so that if we believe in Him, follow Him, ask for forgiveness from Him, we can have eternal life that we do not deserve! The Gospel- What real love is!

Let us not forget the true meaning of love. Dare to be loved with the love that only God can give us-the love that never ends, never changes, and never gives up on us.

Day 65
Dare to Surrender

"I HAVE BEEN CRUCIFIED WITH CHRIST. IT IS NO LONGER I WHO LIVE."
GALATIANS 2:20

CS Lewis said, "The more we let God take over us, the more we become ourselves."

Sometimes, the word surrender has quite negative connotations, especially in Northern Irish culture. The very word can put fear in people, especially when talking about surrendering our whole lives to God. I used to think that surrender meant losing all of me and being reduced to a shell who blindly followed God. Then I realised just how much of God's power can be harnessed by deciding to surrender all of ourselves over to Him. Surrendering to God takes the pressure off me having to decide what to do with my life and gives the decisions over to God. By surrendering to God, we become who we are truly meant to be instead of faking, putting on a mask, trying to stumble around, looking for what we are meant to become.

Many people do not surrender everything to God because they do not know God. They have a fear of giving over control of their lives to a God they do not know. They do not understand what we mean when we say allow God to control your life. The Bible says in Romans 6:20 that we have "left the kingdom of darkness and are now slaves to righteousness". I am someone who struggled with this, thinking that control meant bondage and destruction.

Surrendering to God is not about control in a worldly way; this is about God's control. God will never hurt you or use this control for a power trip, but only to give you a promising future. God is good, God is perfect, and God is love. He will never use our vulnerable surrender state against us, but always for our good and His Glory.

God can and will ask you to do many complex things when you surrender your life to Him. Look at Abraham and Isaac and Jesus in

the garden of Gethsemane. It is not easy doing some of the things God asks of me when I surrender to Him. But when you know your God, and you know His heart, you understand that His ways are higher than your ways and His thoughts above your thoughts. So you start to be able to see things from Heaven's perspective instead of your own.

I know my God will never hurt me, fail me, reject me, undermine me, leave me behind, forget me, or be disappointed or ashamed of me. Even if I fail, He will never have those feelings toward me. Get to know GOD. Get to actually know Him. Surrendering your life to Him will be a more straightforward thing because you become aware that He is the best person to take control of it. And so surrender becomes easy for you because you want God to have control of it. You now have a relationship instead of a friendship with God, and that makes all the difference.

Dare to surrender your life to a God who loves and cares for you, and you could begin to make a significant impact on this world and the devils kingdom!

Day 66
Dare to follow

"FOR WE ARE HIS WORKMANSHIP, CREATED IN CHRIST JESUS FOR GOOD WORKS, WHICH GOD PREPARED BEFOREHAND THAT WE SHOULD WALK IN THEM."
EPHESIANS 2:10

When we surrender all we have to God, as we discussed in yesterday's devotion, God will begin to lay out the plans and purposes that He has for us. I do not know if you have ever realised before that you are made on purpose, for a purpose- You are! When you begin to follow Christ, you realise what that purpose is and what God's bigger plan for you is.

Many people automatically think that surrendering means going to Africa or faraway places, and if you don't go there, you aren't fully offered to God. And yes, sometimes God may ask you to go to the deepest parts of the world where He needs you to work. But just as equally surrendering is willing to stay precisely where you are when He tells you to and do what He asks right then and there.

God will only ever ask you to use what you have, never what you don't. He used a staff of Moses', a small boy's lunch, a jawbone of a donkey, a plumb-line, a tree, and the Bible says over and over he uses the weak and foolish things of the world. This means He can use you and me, and whatever we have, we bring to Him is all He asks of us.

God has placed you where you are, with the people in your world, for a reason. Choose to cross over roads when you hear Him whisper, speak up when you hear Him tell you to, start to go outside of your comfort zone for Him, and He will begin to do amazing things. You begin to harness God's power and see Him at work in your life when you start to surrender everything over to Him, willing to do whatever whenever for His Kingdom's cause.

When you walk over to someone and open your mouth and start to speak, that's when you gain victory over the Devil, that's when God's power comes upon you, and that's when you see miracles happen.

Dare to follow God with everything you have and see the difference in your world, in you and those around.

Day 67
Dare to Gain

"I APPEAL TO YOU, THEREFORE, BROTHERS BY THE MERCIES OF GOD, TO PRESENT YOUR BODIES AS A LIVING SACRIFICE, HOLY AND ACCEPTABLE TO GOD."
ROMANS 12:1

I want to leave you with the knowledge that there are benefits to surrender that far outweigh the price it costs us to offer our lives to God. Let's look at these and see what benefits are accessible to us when we surrender our entire lives to God.

We have **power**- Joshua, at the battle of Jericho, fell on his face before God and surrendered the plans he had to the seemingly crazy plan God gave him. That surrender led to a tremendous victory. In Acts 2, the disciples had sacrificed all to Jesus, and then the power came upon them from on high, and God transformed thousands of people's lives. Power comes from surrender. When we surrender our plans to God, we experience victory over battles we have been fighting in our lives, challenges we face, obstacles in our pathway- all can be defeated through the power we gain from surrender.

We have **peace**- It says in Job 22:21, "Agree with God and be at peace." Ever tried to argue with God? You can't sleep right or think right, but when you surrender all over to Him, you get that peace that goes beyond any understanding and never goes away.

We have **freedom**- Romans 6:17 (NIV) "Offer yourselves up to God and the freedom never quits." What a life you could have where freedom never quits, where sin and the Devil are constantly defeated in your life because you do whatever God asks you to do without arguing or bargaining. We often push aside a wonderful life when we try to do things your way.

We have **joy**- not happiness. There is a difference. Happiness comes and goes; joy is constant and more profound, and with a

135

knowledge that even if circumstances go wrong, God is in control.

Surrender brings joy. Surrendering all to God means that you are giving God reign in the good and the bad, and that means you have freedom from fear, confusion, or pressure because it is on God.

Dare to surrender all to God, dare to follow Him completely, and dare to gain the benefits. You will see differences in yourself and those around you, and you will start to make an impact on this world!

Day 68
Dare to Walk

"EVEN THOUGH I WALK THROUGH THE VALLEY OF THE SHADOW OF DEATH, I WILL FEAR NO EVIL FOR YOU ARE WITH ME; YOUR ROD AND YOUR STAFF THEY COMFORT ME."
PSALM 23:4

My daughter Hannah loves me being beside her when we are out for a walk. I provide comfort, security, love, support, help and closeness. How much more does our Heavenly Father want to give us all these things, especially in our darkest times. God wants to help you personally, not be a far-off God looking at you struggling through the dark pathways of life. He wants to walk alongside you as you go through it.

Death, fear and loss are no longer the painful enemies to me that they used to be before I became a Christian, because Jesus took the total weight of sin on the cross, including death that came along with that sin. He defeated death and fear and hopelessness fully and completely when He rose from the dead for anyone with a relationship with Him. So now, anyone in a relationship with Jesus no longer has to fear death as they once did. It is just a shadow, not the real thing.

Let me tell you about shadows, however, they can't hurt you, but they can darken your world for a while. And it would be wrong for us to act as if they didn't. Shadows can also leave you feeling vulnerable. Have you ever walked down a dark shadowy path that is unknown to you? It can be scary and fearful, and you lack the security you used to have in the light. You can feel so powerless when you're alone in that place.

In the original language, the word 'comfort' here means a feeling of security. It is not as comfortable as sitting, stroking your back, and empathising with you. The word here means that God can give you back that feeling of security you have lost which has left you feeling vulnerable. This comfort is a 'get up and go' comfort because He is with us.

God doesn't expect us to rush through this valley. It says walk. God understands that we all need time. Walking gives the impression to the reader that it is slow, steady, consistent and unhurried. Be patient with yourself and give yourself time to process what has happened; go slowly, talk and ask for help.

However it is walking, it isn't somewhere you stay. There is movement here. David gives us the impression that we don't live here. We move through to the other side. God offers us help and support, and strength to do this.

Dare to walk even though it is painful. You are not on your own. You have a God who helps, supports and comforts you, and He will help you through.

Day 69
Dare to Love

"LOVE THE LORD YOUR GOD WITH ALL YOUR HEART AND WITH ALL YOUR SOUL AND WITH ALL YOUR MIND."
MATTHEW 22:37

We were walking into the house when Emily suddenly put her head down on my shoulder and proclaimed, "I love you, mummy." It was barely louder than a whisper, but I heard it, and it meant the world to me! She had never told me that she loved me before; she was only nineteen months old, after all.

The first declaration of love is always special to whoever hears it- be it a toddler telling a parent or a boyfriend telling a girlfriend. However, sometimes it is the consistent declarations that are even more precious. I remember my Grandparents dancing together as if they were first dating- a declaration of love after forty years of marriage.

I can only imagine God's heart when someone declares their love to Him for the first time. The Bible tells us in Luke 15:7, "Just so, I tell you, there will be more joy over one sinner who repents than over ninety-nine righteous persons who need no repentance." So much joy, so much celebration over one person who tells God that they love Him and want to follow Him with their whole being. Maybe, all of Heaven could be celebrating over you today if you have never begun that relationship with God before.

If you do not have a relationship with God, the Father's eyes have been scanning the horizon, looking for you, just as he did in the story of the prodigal son (Luke 15:11-32). If you return, as the son did, Father God will welcome you back and celebrate you being home. He would throw a party over the fact that you told Him you loved Him.

Maybe you have followed and loved God for many years already. Do not stop telling Him or showing Him that you love

139

Him. The Bible says we are to love God with our whole being, every bit of us, not because we have to, but because of all He has done for us. That is not a burden on us but a privilege. In your devotions, why not take some time to tell God you love Him again? Instead of just listing our problems to Him, take some time and pour out your devotion to Him. He never stops showing us how much He loves us. Even a whisper of devotion will cause Heaven to celebrate!

Dare to love. Dare to show God how much you love Him and see the impact it makes on your life when you declare it for the first time or anew.

Day 70
Dare to know your enemy

"YOUR HEART WAS PROUD BECAUSE OF YOUR BEAUTY; YOU CORRUPTED YOUR WISDOM FOR THE SAKE OF YOUR SPLENDOUR. I CAST YOU TO THE GROUND."
EZEKIEL 28:17

"Know thy enemy, and know thyself and in a hundred battles you will never be defeated," is a Chinese proverb from General Sun Tzu. Getting to know your enemy has always been something that sets you up for a more successful battle and a more significant victory.

Let's spend a short time getting to know our enemy before we look over the next few days at how to defeat him. Did you know that Satan was once an angel who served God? More than just an angel, the Bible says in Ezekiel 28 and Isaiah 14:12 that Satan was one of the highest angels. He was one of the two angels closest to God out of all the angels. He was a chosen angel, an anointed angel, and stunningly beautiful. But he wanted more, and he wanted to be like God, so he began to try and overtake God in the heavenly. He managed to turn one-third of all the angels over to his side, so God had to punish him. And he was cast out of his position in God's Heaven, and God created hell for him and all the angels who had followed him! Hell was created for Satan and his angels, not humans.

Why? Because pride had entered his heart, and he was cast out of Heaven because of this. So ever since, Satan has been out to attack those who love God and follow Him. Pride is putting yourself first before anything or anyone else.

He cannot attack God Himself, so Satan attacks us to hurt God as much as possible. He hates that we were created in God's image, so he attacks our bodies and how we view ourselves. He hates that we have been made for a relationship with God and others because he will live eternity in isolation in Hell. So he attacks our relationship with God and one another to ruin the

141

chance to have life in all its fullness. He hates the idea that we can experience freedom in our spiritual life since he is forever condemned, so he tries as much as he can to steal, kill and destroy us (John 10:10) and ruin the freedom God intended for us to have. Our enemy is not very creative, so every attack he goes after Christians with, can always be traced back to pride, putting ourselves before God.

The good news is that we do not need to fear this enemy, because, through Jesus' death on the cross, he has been defeated. We do not need to listen to the enemy because through Jesus' resurrection, he no longer holds the keys to death and Hell. We do not need to follow the enemy's lies because we can hear from God every day and know the right path to take. The good news is the enemy does not need to hold power over us if we follow our God and know His ways. Every trick Satan attempts does not need to succeed because we can be safe with our Heavenly Father if we keep our eyes on Him. It is essential to know our enemy, but we do not need to fear him. Knowing his ways means we can be aware of his traps before they trip us up.

Dare to know your enemy, it will help you fight spiritual warfare more knowledgeably, but we do not fight him with our power. We can depend on God in every battle that we face.

Day 71
Dare to be Prepared

**"THEREFORE TAKE UP THE WHOLE ARMOUR OF GOD THAT YOU MAY BE ABLE TO WITHSTAND IN THE EVIL DAY...STAND THEREFORE, HAVING FASTENED ON THE BELT OF TRUTH."
EPHESIANS 6:13-14**

I remember going paint-balling for my brother's twenty-first birthday party. Before we did anything, we had to dress correctly or we could get badly injured. If you have ever gone paint-balling before, you will understand. We had to put on a helmet and a bulletproof vest, and we had to wear goggles to protect our eyes and correct shoes on our feet. You were not allowed out on the field without each item of protection on you correctly, and it had to stay on the entire time you were on the field, whether you were in the game or not. I still clearly remember the pain I felt and my eyes watering when a bullet hit me square on top of the head, just in between my protective gear, on my vulnerable spot. It was painful and intense.

I am so thankful that God gives us a guide to the armour that we need to wear each day to protect ourselves against the enemy. God does not leave us to fumble around trying to guess what we need, but He has also given it to us to wear.

Paul uses the imagery of a Roman Soldier to depict what we should wear as a Christian to protect us against the enemy's attacks. The first item he describes is the 'belt of truth.' The Roman Soldiers wore their belts constantly as a sign of who they were, even off duty. It was their identity that they belonged to that army. Not only that, but it was where they stored their swords for battle and the other equipment that they needed quickly under attack. It was the item that held their armour together.

The 'belt of truth is the identity that we belong to God. It is our symbol that we are fighting in God's army, for "Everyone who hears my voice, is of truth," Jesus said (John 18:37). Truth can do

143

so much for a Christian. Firstly, the Bible says, 'The Truth shall set you free' (John 8:32). When we do as the Bible says and live as the Bible says we should, there is much freedom to be experienced. We are freed from the path of sin that we used to follow and live the life that God always intended us to live.

Truth can also offer us protection. The Bible says, 'Your Word is a lamp to my feet and a light to my path" (Psalm 119:105). When we know the truth of God's word, we do not have to stagger and guess the pathway ahead because God clearly shows us in His Word.

The belt of truth is the thing that all other aspects of our armour hang from. We need it to use God's Word correctly in battle, identify ourselves as part of God's army, know the right path for our lives, and stand against the enemy. Put on your belt of truth today- learn the Word of God, learn how to use it correctly, and put it into action in your life. Never be without it as we go about our daily life.

Dare to be prepared by fastening the belt of truth, the first part of the armour of God.

Day 72
Dare to be prepared
"AND HAVING PUT ON THE BREASTPLATE OF RIGHTEOUSNESS."
EPHESIANS 6:14

Paul's depiction of the armour of God continues with the image of a breastplate of righteousness which the believer should clothe himself with. To fully understand what Paul was insinuating here, we again need to look at the armour worn by the soldier on the day he was writing.

The breastplate the Romans wore was a large metal sheet that entirely covered the soldier from the shoulder to the groin. There were many more miniature metal sheets joined together to cover him at every side from every angle to ensure the enemy did not easily target his vital organs. It allowed them to be protected against any unexpected or overwhelming attack his shield may miss.

This is the image Paul wants us to visualise. We need to be fully protected on every side, from every angle, against any unexpected attack from our enemy. We all know that the devil frequently will attack us with the same thing. He is not very creative, and so when he finds your vulnerable point, that is where he will target until you have it covered.

Righteousness, thankfully, does not depend on us. It is not our righteousness that Paul is referring to. The word 'righteousness' means to be morally right or acceptable. We are not within ourselves. Even as Christians, we have faults and fight against ourselves, continually, knowing what we should do and not do.

So, thankfully, God has provided us with righteousness. When we begin a relationship with God, He makes us right with Him, despite all our flaws in ourselves. Thank God!

While the breastplate does not depend on us, 'putting it on' does. We have a responsibility to know how to do this. We must get to know the Word of God and get to know His ways above our own (Matthew 6:33). We must learn to act when God points out an area within us that requires us to change and obey Him. We can learn to spend time hearing His voice and practice doing what He says. All these habits allow us to put on righteousness as a breastplate, so that when the devil comes to attack, we know the Word, we have changed our ways, and we can hear God's voice already.

Dare to be prepared by putting on the breastplate of righteousness, so that in a battle, you are covered with God's righteousness and the Word of God; the enemy's power will be reduced when he comes against God's word instead of ours.

Day 73
Dare to be prepared
"AND AS SHOES FOR YOUR FEET, HAVING PUT ON THE READINESS GIVEN BY THE GOSPEL OF PEACE."
EPHESIANS 6:15

During a battle in Paul's day, the enemy used a dirty tactic to prevent the oncoming opponents from reaching your side of the battlefield. Before the war started, the enemy would go and lay traps throughout the area where the oncoming soldiers had to walk across. They disguised them in the ground, covered with sharp metal traps that would either cripple or kill a soldier whose unshod foot would come upon them. These traps would not be seen by the eye of those running across no man's land, and so it was vital to have your feet shod with the protective shoe provided.

These shoes were not the typical sandals worn by the men of the day; they were only worn by those heading into battle. These shoes were three layers of leather, laced around the ankle with spikes in the sole to hold the foot steady in terrain, which was not easy to walk on. It was essential to wear the right shoes, or you could be maimed and crippled for life if you were caught in the enemy's trap.

Paul here refers to the shoes of the readiness of the Gospel of peace as part of the believers' armour. These are not just any shoes. They are not shoes of hopefulness, shoes of love or even shoes of forgiveness. They are shoes of the readiness of the Gospel of peace.

Here in Greek, the word 'readiness' is *hetoimasia,* which means 'to prepare a firm foundation.' The Gospel is the Christian's firm foundation against any attack from the enemy. The Gospel is the good news that Jesus died for our sins and rose again, that we have righteousness through what Jesus did on the cross, that we have eternal life because of His resurrection, and that we can know peace with God here on earth because of sins forgiven. That is the Gospel of peace.

That Gospel can protect you against every trap the enemy sets for you, against every unfamiliar path you may have to walk, against every obstacle or distraction that may litter our way of life. The Gospel is secure, never changing, it is never-ending, and it is a firm foundation on which we can build our lives. Even more, it is what the enemy hates us repeating more than anything else because it reminds him that he is a defeated foe who has no real power over us when we belong to God.

The Gospel is genuine protection for us throughout the spiritual battle we face. Let us constantly remind ourselves of the Good News Jesus provided us with to stand strong in the battles that we encounter throughout our lives.

Dare to be prepared, put on the sure foundation of the Gospel of peace that will keep your footing protected and secure in all the ups and downs of life.

Day 74
Dare to be prepared

"IN ALL CIRCUMSTANCES, TAKE UP THE SHIELD OF FAITH, WITH WHICH YOU CAN EXTINGUISH ALL THE FLAMING DARTS OF THE EVIL ONE;."
EPHESIANS 6:16

If you are a follower of Christ, you will already have experienced such an arrow that came against you from the enemy. We have a choice to either stand up and fight or believe what he was saying and quit. The arrows from the enemy are not rubber arrows. The enemy arrows in the Roman days were often set on fire to do as much damage as possible if they hit their target. The arrows from our enemy are the same. They are alight with accusation, doubt, confusion, disorder, shame, hurt, bitterness, resentment, or fear. When he fires a flaming dart at the Christian, if it strikes, it can damage, causing pain, suffering, torment, and distress. He loves it because it causes as much pain to God and us as possible, which is his only aim in this world.

That is why the shield was so crucial in battle. The Roman shield, called a scutum, was often as large as a door, and each soldier fitted neatly together with his fellow soldier's shield in battle to form a 'testudo', or tortoiseshell effect. With this effect in place, the enemy arrows found it much harder to penetrate, and the flames were often extinguished as they hit the shield. They were not just a defensive item but could push back the enemy when used correctly.

God knew what He was doing when He created the Church of Jesus Christ so that we could come together as an army with our shields of faith interlocked. If you have a promise from God, I encourage you to tell someone you trust, so that when the enemy comes with flaming darts, you can together stand with your shields raised and extinguish his flames. If you have a promise from God, write it down, so that you can have your shield beside you at all times, and in all circumstances, ready for any unexpected and unprompted attack from the enemy.

Faith provides us with so much that we can fight with. Faith provides us with confidence in things not yet seen (Hebrews 11:1) and the knowledge that we can trust in God even though we cannot yet see things come to pass. It is through faith that we are justified and have peace with God (Romans 5:1), it is through faith that we can have hope (Romans 5:2), and it is through faith that we have victory in our spiritual lives (1 John 5:4).

Faith is our protective barrier against the enemy and all of his attacks. Get to know your Bible and the promises of God. Understand what God is trying to say to you, and it is through the written word of God that we can gain our faith to fight the devil, push him back, and overcome each dart he fires at us.

Dare to be prepared by lifting your shield, sometimes along with someone else, and fight the devil with the word of God and the word of your testimony.

Day 75
Dare to be prepared
"AND TAKE THE HELMET OF SALVATION,"
EPHESIANS 6:17A

No one enjoys wearing a helmet. We bought Hannah her first bicycle not so long ago, and on the way home, we stopped to pick up the helmet for her. She was not a fan of the helmet. It was a bit heavy, uncomfortable and just took time to put on when she wanted to get on her bike and go. However, the helmet is essential to protect all those vital organs inside your skull-your brain, your eyes, your spinal cord all rely on protection should your head get a knock. They are fragile and easily damaged. The Romans knew this, so they had a large helmet made of brass or silver which covered from above their forehead right down their neck, and in battle, they were able to pull this down over their eyes. This ensured that their last line of defence, their helmet, could provide complete protection.

Paul again likens our spiritual armour to the Roman armour. He refers in this verse to the last remaining piece of defensive armour- we have our belt of truth, the breastplate of righteousness, shoes of the Gospel, and now our helmet of salvation. Salvation throughout the Bible is not just used for having your sins forgiven, though that is a part of it. Salvation is the word *Soteria* in the Greek language, meaning deliverance or saving from. It does not just refer to deliverance from sin, but also from negative thoughts, lies, shame, hurt, bitterness, and anything which would hold you back from fully being able to follow God.

The devil is not creative, he uses the same tactics each time. He usually attacks your mind with thoughts that he knows will distract you from following God, lies that he knows will make you question God, and shame that he knows will prevent you from accessing all the power available. So because this is such a way that the devil can pull us down, Paul encourages us to put on the helmet of salvation- the covering of deliverance from every attack of the enemy.

How do we put on this helmet? We can put on this helmet every day when we open the word of God, and act on it in obedience to Christ. We speak the truth over the lies we hear, and we learn what God's word says and apply it to our daily lives. We read and meditate on the truth to claim deliverance available to us. Jesus won this deliverance for us on the cross when He died and at the resurrection when He rose again, so we now have complete access to this.

Dare to be prepared with this final defensive armour. Dare to hope that God has paid for and completely provided every aspect of the spiritual armour that we need. We simply need to apply it every day, and we can experience victory over the powers of darkness in our lives and be capable of living fully the life God intended us to live.

Day 76
Dare to be Prepared
"AND, THE SWORD OF THE SPIRIT, WHICH IS THE WORD OF GOD."
EPHESIANS 6:17B

God only gave us one weapon out of all the armour pieces that He has equipped us with. The rest of the armour is all defence because He knows that we only need one piece of weaponry for an attack to defeat our enemy. He knows the devil plays dirty and that we need defending on every side, but there is one item that we need to defeat him ultimately.

Suppose you know anything about Roman soldiers of the day, you will know that their swords were called the 'gladius.' They had several different types of gladius that they used. In practice, they used a large, heavy kind, and could have practised with this two or three times a day. However, they used a small eighteen-inch gladius when the battle was against their enemy. This one was not meant to hack people but to destroy them in a stabbing action with minimal effort. They were often able to defeat their enemy by using as little as two inches.

In the Greek language, which Paul wrote in, he uses the same imagery. There are two Greek words for 'Word of God.' One was the word, 'Logos', which means God's entire Word, which we refer to as our Bible. There was another word, ' Rhema,' which is God's specific, unique utterance. There is a difference. In the passage referring to the sword of the Spirit, Paul is using the word 'Rhema.'

In other words, Paul means that we are not told to slash and hack at our enemy, but we are to use our war-attacking gladius, our Rhema, our specific Word that we have received from God to defeat our enemy in his attack. Just as the Romans practised with their larger swords two or three times a day, we are to practice with our 'Logos' as much as possible. Read the word of

God every day, if possible. Get it into your heart and mind, and soul so that when the enemy comes, you have your specific, particular word from God to attack and defeat Him.

When God first called me to Bible College to speak in front of people and proclaim the Gospel through writing, I argued with Him that I was incapable and had nothing worth saying. However, in my daily devotionals (Logos), I got my specific word for attack (Rhema) against the enemy. It is found in Exodus 4:12 "Now, therefore go, and I will be with your mouth and teach you what you shall speak." Every time I get up to speak, I quote that verse aloud, both to remind God of His promise and also to conquer the enemy against making me feel insignificant and useless.

You need to have a Rhema in your life to take down the enemy, who constantly attacks you at your most vulnerable points. The way to get it is to study the Logos, the entire word and ask God to point you to your specific Word from Him. Let's not waste our energy hacking and slicing at the enemy; let's get armed with a specific Word that we have to say, and He has to go in Jesus' name.

Dare to be prepared to fight the battle that is coming our way because the enemy is ready, so we need to be too.

Day 77
Dare to suit up
"PRAYING AT ALL TIMES IN THE SPIRIT WITH ALL PRAYER AND SUPPLICATION. TO THAT END, KEEP ALERT WITH ALL PERSEVERANCE, MAKING SUPPLICATION FOR ALL THE SAINTS." EPHESIANS 6:18

Often this aspect of the spiritual armour is skipped over or not included. However, it is an essential piece required to hold all the other armour elements together. Coupled with receiving a Word or 'Rhema' from the Spirit to attack the enemy, we need to pray in the Spirit to conquer the enemy and cover us completely.

I once heard that a rugby match has the same impact on your body as three car crashes all at the same time. The stress and strain take some time to recover from, and there is an element of rest required once a match is over before they attempt another run. If they wandered into another game without the correct rest for their body, they would easily be overcome.

Similarly, spiritual warfare can dramatically impact your body and your spirit, and there is some recovery time needed. I am not referring to everyday war, but intense spiritual warfare where there has been a direct attack from the enemy. Recovery does not come in eating oranges and having ice baths but in prayer. Prayer for the Christian has a similar impact on the Spirit as an ice bath has on the body- it helps with recovery by relaxing spiritual muscles that have been exercised dramatically.

Prayer is required before, during and after an attack on your spirit, so it is essential to practice. Today's verse reminds us that we are to 'keep alert'. Do not let your guard down, no matter how good your life appears to be. Practice going to God and speaking to Him about everything in your world. Practice going and asking God for cover in the areas you know are vulnerable to attack. Maybe you struggle with insecurity, negative thoughts,

155

or shame- ask God to cover those areas, making it difficult for the enemy to strike directly in those areas in your life.

Prayer is essential to the armour. While we have looked at the armour - the belt, the breastplate, the shoes, the helmet, the sword and prayer - let us take time to pray over ourselves and see the areas where we are most vulnerable. Maybe you are good at having your helmet on but not so good at the belt of truth each day. Or you may find it easy to have your shoes on, but not so much your shield of faith. Pray and ask God where you are exposed and ask Him to cover you and shield you, help you become more aware of it daily, and take it to Him. Thank God we have armour to wear to defeat our enemy in each attack he brings.

We not only have armour, but we also have our God who is fighting and praying for us constantly even though we cannot see Him. Do not give in to an attack. God is with us, helping and providing power when we are at our weakest. The devil is a defeated foe, but he still can influence us if we let him. Let's be a Church that puts our armour on daily, so we can be soldiers fit for battle at a moment's notice.

Dare to be prepared and know that you can win the battle you will face.

Day 78
Dare to Serve

"AS EACH HAS RECEIVED A GIFT, USE IT TO SERVE ONE ANOTHER, AS GOOD STEWARDS OF GOD'S VARIED GRACE."
1 PETER 4:10

If writing this devotional has taught me anything, it is essential to use your gifts to serve each other. I know I have skills in certain areas; however, I know for sure that does not include an eye for detail. I am a big picture type of person. I can see how to do it and get it done without looking at the little details that often make a massive impact on the finished product. I am so thankful I have a good friend with an eye for detail who offered to use her gifts to help me write this book. She saw things I would never have noticed if I had read it three times over!

I also know one of my strengths is not in technology. My husband has a substantial gift for using technology and helped me with the design and formatting. I struggled to do any more than type out this document.

My name may be on the front cover, but it took a lot more than me to get this book out. Your Pastor's name may be on your church billboard, but it takes a lot more than him to reach the community you live in. You may never stand in a pulpit or sing in the band, but it takes more than the people at the forefront to reach everyone for Jesus. That is why we are encouraged to use our gifts to serve others.

Dare to serve others with your gifting. You have a gift your pastor or youth leader or gym instructor or teacher or nurse or tradesman does not have, but they may need it in their life. There is a story that Jesus told about three people who received talents. Two used their talents and multiplied them, and one hid their talent. Never hide your talent.

You may think it is nothing significant, but someone in the Church of Jesus needs it! It may be something that comes naturally to you, but someone else struggles with it. Sometimes we find it hard to see our natural gift from God so don't be afraid to ask others for their advice and what they can see in you. Sometimes it takes someone else to show us where we can serve others the best so be prepared to listen.

Dare to serve others with the gifts that you have received so that you can be a good steward of God's grace! Some people need you, and it's time to stop hiding and start multiplying your gifts.

Day 79
Dare to be Loved

"BUT GOD, BEING RICH IN MERCY, BECAUSE OF THE GREAT LOVE WITH WHICH HE LOVED US, EVEN WHEN WE WERE DEAD IN OUR TRESPASSES, MADE US ALIVE."
EPHESIANS 2:4-5

I was twenty-two years old when I gave my life to Jesus. I had been brought up in a Christian home, but I had never accepted Jesus for myself. To me, it was mostly about rules and regulations, doing what you are told, and as a bit of a rebel, the lifestyle did not seem to suit me. I wanted to do things my way, and I wanted to experience life for myself, so I went the wrong way for quite a while until I gave my life to God. This verse sums up perfectly why I eventually gave my life over because I realised God loved me!

This love that the verse speaks of is great. The word 'great' is *pollen,* which means much or extreme to almost hurting. This great love with which God loved us is an extravagant, outrageous love that could only be given to us by God, especially as the previous verses in this passage were referring to who we were before Christ. We were dead in our sins, following our path for our life, doing our own thing. We were far away from God- But God. But God can step in and transform you because of the extravagant love with which He loved us! How amazing!

The word love is the Greek word *agapao,* which means unconditional love. Love is not love based on the goodness of the beloved or upon natural emotion. Instead, this is benevolent love that constantly seeks out the good of the loved. It is this type of love that God loves us with. Have you accepted this love in your life yet? Have you exchanged your thoughts that a relationship with God is all about religion, to realise it is about a relationship based on eternal, unchanging love for you?

This is not ordinary human love that can come and go or change depending on a mood. It is not a power-based love that can be possessive or controlling. It is a pure, eternal love that is interested only in your good and brings with it life in all its fullness available for all who accept. However, it is our responsibility to decide to lay our life down and follow Jesus because He loves us with this great love. He does not force this love upon us, we must decide to accept it and allow it to transform us.

Dare to allow yourself to be loved by God, and it will transform your life.

Day 80
Dare to be changed

"FOR THE WORD OF GOD IS LIVING AND ACTIVE, SHARPER THAN ANY TWO-EDGED SWORD, PIERCING TO THE DIVISION OF SOUL AND OF SPIRIT, OF JOINTS AND OF MARROW, AND DISCERNING THE THOUGHTS AND INTENTIONS OF THE HEART."
HEBREWS 4:12

Have you ever been reading the Bible, and suddenly a verse or a phrase jumps off the page and catches your attention as if it was just written for you? It is accurate when people claim that the Bible is historical. It was written across 1500 years written by 40 different men. It captures factually correct accounts of Biblical events, which you can check against other historical documents. It is a fact that there was a man named Jesus who lived in Nazareth. It is factual that there was a man named Jonah who went to Nineveh to spread the news of Jesus. It is correct that Herod beheaded John the Baptist. An empty tomb and an ark coincide with the Biblical stories. The Bible is a historical document.

However, unlike any other document that keeps accounts, the Bible is not only factual and living and breathing because it is the Word of God who is very much alive. Therefore, the Bible can speak to us today since it is alive. It can give us a helpful word when we face difficulties or a corrective comment when we are going against what God wants; it can teach us how to live the way God intended, and it can allow us to search for answers when we do not know which way to go.

The Bible is alive, and the Word of God, this verse suggests, is sharp and quick like a sword. God's Word can be swift to get the point across, sharp to prick our conscience and piercing to allow even the most hidden of secrets to be brought into the Light.

Begin to read it for yourself each day as part of a habit. If you haven't already done it, set aside time to listen to what God has

161

to say to you through it. As with any living person, the fantastic thing about the Bible is that we can apply it individually to each circumstance we face. God knows what we need to hear, God knows what we need to survive in this world and so He has provided everything we need in His Word. The Bible says if you are a Christian you can no longer just feed your body to stay alive, but you must also feed your spirit with the food God provides us with, the Bible.

Just as physical food allows our body to grow and stay healthy, allows our cells to work properly and our systems to stay regulated, so spiritual food from the Bible allows us to grow spiritually, stay healthy and know what God wants from us. The Bible tells us what to do in different situations in our life and helps the spiritual part of our body to stay in tune with God.

Dare to be changed by, read, listen to, and use the Bible in your life and see what a difference it makes to you every day.

Day 81
Dare to be an example

LET NO ONE DESPISE YOU FOR YOUR YOUTH, BUT SET THE BELIEVERS AN EXAMPLE IN SPEECH, IN CONDUCT, IN LOVE, IN FAITH, IN PURITY.
1 TIMOTHY 4:12

I love how God incorporates all ages of people in the BIble. Moses and Noah were older men when they began their mission for God. Though maybe called when younger, Joshua and David were middle-aged, when they started to be used by God, including Jesus Himself, who began His ministry when He was thirty-three. Then there is Jeremiah and Timothy, who we are told were young when they started their work for God, possibly teenagers, along with Mary, the mother of Jesus, who is presumed to be in her teens, she had one of the greatest missions in the world cast upon her.

I love how the Bible excludes no one, and God used even the young children to teach the older congregation members. So, whatever age you may be when reading this, know that you are never too old or too young to be used by God. All of us are younger than someone more senior, either spiritually or physically. We all have someone we can look up to and someone who makes us feel like a child in the faith.

So I want to encourage each of us to accept this challenge that Paul put forward to Timothy as our own- set the believers an example in speech, conduct, love, faith and purity. How about that for a challenge to us all? Set an example in speech. The Bible says, "Let your speech always be gracious, seasoned with salt, so that you may know how you ought to answer each person" (Colossians 4:6). The challenge is never to be so overcome with anger or passion that you lose your graciousness toward other believers.

Set an example in conduct and love, as it says in Mark 12:31, to love your neighbour as you love yourself. Putting others before ourselves is an example of behaviour and devotion to the Church, helping those who do not deserve it and being faithful in the small things which God sets before us. All examples of conduct and love to the believers. The final challenge Paul gives is faith and purity. We are to live as a Church that sets Jesus as their example of living a life full of faith and completely pure. He never once faltered or failed in any challenge or task He faced, but committed everything to God in prayer and acting on anything God placed in front of Him.

Set an example to the believers in your world, no matter what age bracket you fall into. Younger members need older members and vice versa. The Church needs each other, and we need people sold out to God to show that it is possible.

Dare to be that example in your world- you could be the beginning of a group of people sold out to God because you took a stand and followed God.

Day 82
Dare to take steps
"THE HEART OF MAN PLANS HIS WAY, BUT THE LORD ESTABLISHES HIS STEPS."
PROVERBS 16:9

I am a big picture type of person. I always have been. I see a project or plan that needs to be done, and I attack it with gusto. I often begin a project without fully stopping and thinking it through. For example, I began to write this devotional book because I knew it needed to be done, and I wanted to do it. So I started and wrote ninety days worth of devotions in one month. However, there were a lot of corrections to be made to my writing style to make it ready for publishing. There was proofreading, editing, designing, and formatting to make it worthy of people reading and understanding. There were steps to be taken in my big picture of a devotional book which I was not prepared for. There were a lot of actions to be taken in my overall plan, which I did not enjoy. I was not too fond of editing, and I wouldn't say I liked proofreading. I saw a project and wanted it done, but some steps needed to be taken for my book to work and be used by God.

We often do not appreciate these steps. We like to see a finished project; we may even enjoy the big picture of getting it done until we look at the steps. Steps can be challenging, dull, monotonous and complex. One big jump is more straightforward and sometimes even more exciting than taking steps. Ask anyone in a gym; taking steps is one of the best ways to burn calories because they are hard work.

Yet, steps are essential. This verse explains how often we determine a plan, but God establishes the steps. The Lord enables the project to be done, but there is a pathway that we must take for the plan to be achieved in God's way so he can effectively use it. We do not always appreciate those steps or even count them necessary, but they are the way that God provides for us to take. We can either choose to go His way or go about things our way.

Maybe today you are planning something, or God has given you a vision for work in His kingdom. It can seem exciting, and we are all in until we begin to look at the steps. Don't quit on the stairway. God has a reason for taking you that way; He has a method in the apparent chaos that sometimes we face when we do things God's way instead of our own. Moses maybe had other plans than crossing through a vast, deep, fast-paced sea, but God wanted His power to be displayed. Jonah did not want to go to Nineveh, but God wanted a city to be saved. Esther had not planned on becoming queen, but God wanted to keep a nation. Mary wanted to be married, but God wanted to use her in His plan to save the world.

Dare to take steps, even if they do not make sense to you. God will use your big plan in a far more excellent way than you could ever imagine if you take the steps that He has planned for you.

Day 83
Dare to Pray

"REJOICE ALWAYS, PRAY WITHOUT CEASING, GIVE THANKS IN ALL CIRCUMSTANCES, FOR THIS IS THE WILL OF GOD IN CHRIST JESUS FOR YOU."
1 THESSALONIANS 5:16-18

I have a mirror that is particularly special to me- I call it my prayer mirror. It is in our bedroom, and in lipstick around it are written initials of people I pray for every day. I find it helpful as I dress in the morning and head to bed at night, to have this as a reminder to pray. It's nothing special; it is just an aid to help me remember to bring people before God every day.

Prayer can be tricky. It can often feel like our words are bouncing off the wall, speaking to thin air. It can often feel like we aren't gaining any ground and are alone in our struggles. Sometimes it can feel like what we are repeatedly praying for never seems to get answered, and we start to lose faith in the battle.

And so, I want to remind you that He hears you. In the many prayers you have cried out to Him, He hears you. In the many hours you have spent pleading for your prodigal to come home, He hears you. In the many nights you have lain awake and poured out your anxieties to Him, He hears you.

Your prayers are more than words, more than an end of day attitude; they are more than talking to yourself. The Almighty God who can perform miracles, who can do the impossible, who understands you and sees you and knows you is listening to you.

Many of us are here today because people prayed. So many of us are healthy because people prayed, and you may be the answer to someone else's prayers. So keep going, keep praying, and keep believing.

Write on your mirror, journal, write prayer notes, and have an accountability partner. Your prayers make a difference! The book of Daniel talks about how people's prayers were the breakthrough method. If we only realised how much power was in prayer, we would be down on our knees so much more!

Dare to pray because God hears you. He heard you before. He hears you now. Keep praying, keep believing, and keep going. I can only imagine getting to Heaven and someday seeing the difference our prayers on earth made in the spiritual realm.

Day 84
Dare to Knock

"SO, PETER WAS KEPT IN PRISON, BUT EARNEST PRAYER FOR HIM WAS MADE TO GOD BY THE CHURCH."
ACTS 12:5

"Mummy, can I have..." is a very common phrase in our home. With two girls who have active imaginations, I frequently get asked if I can join in a game or bring out the crayons, or go up and play in the tent. Even if I say, 'no' to one request, this does not put them off asking again!

Sometimes, in our spiritual life, we can be easily deterred if we receive a 'no' from God to our prayers. If God does not meet our expectations, we can be put off from asking again, we can think He doesn't love us, or we can even start to doubt His power. If God has not answered our prayers the way we hoped He would, we can so often decide to quit so our hopes and expectations are not dashed again.

The church in Acts 12 was praying earnestly for Peter to be released from prison. I can imagine the prayers were intense and consistent and they did not stop asking, however, I never noticed before that the church in Acts 12 had already received a 'no' from God to their previous prayer.

It mentions at the start of Acts 12 that James the apostle was imprisoned and had his head chopped off. I am sure the church had just been praying earnestly for James too. Yet, God decided not to answer their prayers the way they had asked for James and took him home to be with God instead.

The church could have easily given up praying for Peter when James was beheaded and said that God did not care, God couldn't do what they asked, their prayers made no difference to anyone- sound familiar? I often think like that when God does not answer my prayers the way I want him too. Yet, the church kept knocking, waiting for God to answer them. They had faith that exceeded their circumstances, they had knowledge about God that superseded their own opinions and they had determination to look beyond their experiences to the truth of God's Word which said to keep knocking despite the circumstances.

I would love to become a prayer warrior, like the people in the first century church. How much more powerful would we be if we kept believing in God no matter what we had been through, no matter what the results, no matter what the previous answer had been. How much more effective would our prayers be if we stopped looking at our circumstances and focused on our God. Today we could begin. We could begin to come to God with more faith than we did yesterday, begin to bring our problems to Him believing that He can help us, and begin to ask, expecting an answer to come. This first century church did not stop knocking Heaven's door with their prayers even though they were having a tough time.

Let us become a people who will dare to keep knocking, dare to persevere, no matter what we face. If the devil cannot stop us with discouragement, we will be a people he will fear.

Day 85
Dare to Confess

"BUT IF WE CONFESS OUR SINS, HE IS FAITHFUL AND JUST TO FORGIVE US OUR SINS AND TO CLEANSE US FROM ALL UNRIGHTEOUSNESS."
1 JOHN 1:9

``Confession is good for the soul" is an Old Scottish Proverb that you may have heard before. Perhaps, unknown to the author of such a proverb, that quote holds its roots in this Bible verse, and we could say it is a bit underwhelming considering what the verse says. The Bible states that confession is not just good for the soul, it cleanses the soul and allows all our sins to be forgiven. My former self had a lot of sins needing forgiveness. I went my own way, did my own thing, and pushed God into the background as I enjoyed my life the way I wanted to. I did not deserve to be forgiven, and I did not deserve any of the benefits that come from being so.

However, in another demonstration of His grace and mercy toward us, Jesus has based complete and total forgiveness solely on the confession of our sins. Admission, by definition, is to acknowledge and disclose our guilt. Jesus does not mean to confess our guilt and sins to the entire world. He has made it possible for all of our sins to be cleansed entirely if we confess our wrongdoing to God Himself, and He is the only one who needs to hear it. How amazing is our God?

We do not need to work for forgiveness or beg God for His mercy. The Bible says we are to confess. That is the only requirement. Tell God that we have done wrong, list them out before Him, and declare that we will turn away from what we have done before. The Bible tells us that He will cleanse us from all unrighteousness in our life- every guilty thought, every wrong deed, every gossiping word and every godless act-God rids our life of them all as if we had never done them before. Jesus took our place on the Cross, and He took each sinful act upon Himself so that we can be thoroughly cleansed from everything;

we have to confess, and we will receive exceptional forgiveness.

Have you confessed before? Maybe you need to acknowledge it again? We want to keep short accounts with God if we follow Him, so confession should be daily, as few of us can make it through a day without a confession to make at the end. The fantastic news is available to everyone; all you need to do is dare to confess.

Dare to confess to God and benefit from a clean conscience and a cleansed soul.

Day 86
Dare to be brave

"AND YOU WILL HEAR OF WARS AND RUMOURS OF WARS. SEE THAT YOU ARE NOT ALARMED, FOR THIS MUST TAKE PLACE, BUT THE END IS NOT YET...ALL THESE ARE BUT THE BEGINNING OF THE BIRTH PAINS."
MATTHEW 24:6,8.

I remember the feeling of being told that I was moving to delivery to birth both my babies. Hannah was at the end of 29 hours, Emily was only 8 hours. If you have ever been in a delivery room you will know the events that unfold. There is toil, there is screaming, there seems to be unbearable pain and you wonder what the point of it all is. Until the birth happens. Then there is usually perfect joy and peace.

Birth brings new life.

Jesus Himself left a message for His Church in Matthew 24. He said (and I paraphrase) when wars begin, and rumours of wars start, don't be alarmed! These are the beginning of birth pains. Birth pains which, yes will be hard and painful and almost unbearable to endure at times, but will lead us to new life. Eternal life. Our Kings return.

We have watched the news enough times to know that there are wars beginning throughout this world. I have watched videos of bombs dropping and children screaming. I hugged my girls tight thankful that we are safe.

But through it all I heard Jesus' words as well, "do not be alarmed."

The Greek word "alarmed" used here is only used in the Bible with regard to the end times. There is a desperation to this word. A fear associated with it. Not alarmed as in, 'I've lost my keys'. Alarmed as in fear for your life. There is a noise associated with this word. The noise of the Church crying out in fear. Jesus knew that the wars that would begin in the end times could cause His Church to fear to the point of absolute panic and become so distracted we loose the point of what is going on. So He left us this message. For us. For today.

(I paraphrase) Don't be so scared of all that is going around you that you forget where all of this is leading to. It is leading to His return. And that is always our source of hope.

A hope that never shakes no matter what the news says. A hope that never breaks no matter what the videos show. A hope that never dies no matter what the wars bring. A hope that never fades no matter how desperate life feels. A hope that is so strong it can literally break the fear of death itself. A hope that is so powerful you can still see love in the midst of hatred. A hope that is so consistent it brings stability in the midst of uncertain futures. The hope whose name is Jesus our King who knows the end from the beginning and is never taken by surprise, calls to us "Do not be alarmed! New life is coming!!"

Dare to be brave in the midst of uncertain and fearful times, God is still in control.

Day 87
Dare to be vulnerable

"SINCE THEN, WE HAVE A GREAT HIGH PRIEST WHO HAS PASSED THROUGH THE HEAVENS, JESUS, THE SON OF GOD."
HEBREWS 4:14

I sat in the paediatric emergency room with our youngest daughter, waiting for the doctor's report. Her gasps for breath that morning had warned me something was not right, and so we sat in room three in the emergency department, waiting to hear why her airways were constricting. It was a difficult moment trying to deal with an uncomfortable, tired, sick one-year-old on my own while trying to stay calm and responsive to her needs. It was at that moment, while she was gasping in my ear and crying with a rasp that sounded like a grate was in her throat, that I began to pray. I began to pray aloud to the great High Priest, who I know sits on the throne. I began to pray to the One I knew could heal, and who knew what was going on in my daughter's body better than any doctor. I prayed with confidence in my spirit even though it wasn't in my voice, because I knew I could trust God to do what was right for us. I made myself vulnerable because I knew I couldn't do anything for her myself.

Sometimes we need to see God again for who He is. He is not an older man sitting in Heaven, unable to help us or hear our call. He is also not a magician who waves a wand to give us exactly what we want every time we pray. God is a God who is described as our high priest. When Paul wrote this, the high priest went to God on behalf of the people and brought the people's requests and confessions before God. Hebrews 7:25 says that Jesus is living to make intercession for us before the Father. When I prayed for Emily, Jesus prayed for me to the Father. When you are facing a difficulty, or a challenge, or need help, Jesus is praying for you before the Father.

Prayer changes lives, situations, circumstances and raises hope in the darkest of situations. When we pray, we do not bounce words off the wall, but we activate Heaven's armies to fight with us and for us. When we pray, we call to the living God who is higher, stronger and more powerful than anyone else we can call on. When we pray, we admit that we can do nothing and need God to come and help us in what we face. But we need to be vulnerable and allow God into the most painful parts of our lives sometimes.

We have a high priest who has lived as we have, who has been where we are, walked how we walk, faced what we face, and can pray for us before the Father with clarity and passion because He loves us. He wants you to approach Him and come to Him, so He can show you how much He loves you.

Dare to be vulnerable with what you need from the Father because He can help you. Be vulnerable and see how God will not expose it in your life but will protect you, help you and leave you feeling safe and loved through it all.

Day 88
Dare to begin again
"FOR BY (FAITH) THE PEOPLE OF OLD RECEIVED THEIR COMMENDATION."
HEBREWS 11:2

I love the Hall of Faith in Hebrews 11. It is full of people who we know in the Bible, spiritual giants, and the chapter recounts their great deeds of faith. I love reading all the included people, partly to encourage myself rather than admire their work. I am inspired through it all because instead of being a chapter about unattainable people, it makes faith that pleases God entirely within reach.

Many people in the hall of faith have messed up throughout their lives. Noah got drunk after building the ark and disgraced himself in front of his sons. Abraham lost faith and decided to do things his way, which led to two nations that have been in conflict ever since. Sarah encouraged Abraham to rush ahead of God and laughed when God made her a promise. Moses was refused entry to the promised land because he lost his temper, and Samson was left blind because of his pride. Yet, they are all included in this great chapter which praises them for their faith and commitment to God.

Maybe today, you have counted yourself out of being included by God in His plan. Perhaps you started following God and have made mistakes along the way, choosing to take yourself out and declaring you are no longer of any use. I challenge you, dare to begin again. Dare to recommit your life to God again and start to be of service to Him in His kingdom. Do not let the devil take you out of being used in God's plan because of a past mistake you may have made. Satan wants you to believe that once you make a mistake, you are of no use in God's kingdom anymore. Do not believe him.

I am so thankful this passage is included in the Bible because many spiritual warriors stories end with their failure and disgrace. However, here, we can see how faithful they are and how much of a difference they made because they were committed. Time is too short, and your purpose is too great for the enemy to hold you back with a failure in your life.

No matter what you have done so far, go to God and confess, recommit your life to Him, and begin again. We can all be included in God's plan if we dare to begin again.

Day 89
Dare to run

"THEREFORE, SINCE WE ARE SURROUNDED BY SO GREAT A CLOUD OF WITNESSES, LET US ALSO LAY ASIDE EVERY WEIGHT AND SIN WHICH CLINGS SO CLOSELY AND LET US RUN WITH ENDURANCE THE RACE THAT IS SET BEFORE US."
HEBREWS 12:1

If you have ever watched the Olympics, you will have seen the great crowds that stand around the stadium watching and applauding the competitors. You will have seen the coaches on the side looking stressed and anxious until the event is over and then hugging and clapping the competitor they have coached for so long. You will have seen the determination on people's faces as they begin a race, crouched and ready to run at the gun. They have trained for this, and they do not stop until they cross that finish line.

This is the imagery that Paul is attempting to leave us within Hebrews, that of a champion running a race set before him with a crowd of people cheering him on as he runs. Of course, it is not a physical race but the spiritual race God has entrusted to us. I love to picture this imagery, the witnesses who have gone on before us to Heaven, who have already reached their reward, cheering us on to keep going and keep fighting the fight because they know what is before us. They understand fully the price Christ paid for us, and they know it is all worth it.

I don't workout. I tried it once and discovered I did not like it! However, if I know one thing, it is the power of streamlining yourself to be as aerodynamic as possible. You do not run a race with every piece of clothing you own. You remove as much as possible to make it easier to run and run well.

In the Christian race, Paul is encouraging us to set things aside, to run the race well. He encourages us to take off the weights of burdens that we have carried, shame that we have endured, or hurt that we have faced that have maybe held us back until now.

Take them to the cross of Christ and ask Him to enable you to leave them there so you can run the race well. He persuades us to set aside every sin which could so easily entangle us in this race. The devil knows our vulnerable points and loves to lead us into temptation constantly. The devil is known as 'the thief', and he has an innate desire to steal from you in every possible way. He wants to steal the race that God has set before you by trying to get you to hold on to sin you enjoy, hold on to hurt you have experienced, grudges you have had for years so that you cannot run.

Can I encourage you, along with Paul, to set them aside? Go to Jesus and ask for His help. Go to friends and begin to be accountable. Ask for help where you need it to start running this race with endurance. It is not a sprint. It is a long term commitment, and to have perseverance, we have to focus on what matters.

Let us lay aside everything that can hold us back and dare to run. We have a crowd of witnesses cheering us on who know how determined you need to be, and seeing Jesus at the end of the race will be worth it all.

Day 90
Dare to Hope

"THEN THE ANGEL SHOWED ME THE RIVER OF THE WATER OF LIFE, BRIGHT AS CRYSTAL, FLOWING FROM THE THRONE OF GOD AND OF THE LAMB, THROUGH THE MIDDLE OF THE STREET OF THE CITY; ALSO, ON EITHER SIDE OF THE RIVER, THE TREE OF LIFE WITH ITS TWELVE KINDS OF FRUIT, YIELDING ITS FRUIT EACH MONTH. THE LEAVES OF THE TREE WERE FOR THE HEALING OF THE NATIONS. NO LONGER WILL THERE BE ANYTHING ACCURSED, BUT THE THRONE OF GOD AND OF THE LAMB WILL BE IN IT, AND HIS SERVANTS WILL WORSHIP HIM. THEY WILL SEE HIS FACE, AND HIS NAME WILL BE ON THEIR FOREHEADS. AND NIGHT WILL BE NO MORE. THEY WILL NEED NO LIGHT OF LAMP OR SUN, FOR THE LORD GOD WILL BE THEIR LIGHT, AND THEY WILL REIGN FOREVER AND EVER."
REVELATION 22:1-5

I love thinking about Heaven. I love thinking about what lies ahead of us as Christians. The description John has left of Heaven for us is fantastic and allows the imagination to try and conceive just a bit of what lies in store for us. The tremendous news that God has left us with is that earth is not our final resting place, the grave is not the end, death has been defeated, and we have a place in Heaven which Jesus Himself is preparing for us! Not to mention all the loved ones who have gone before us and are already singing the praises of God in incredible worship and splendour.

We can have hope in life beyond this world because God has laid it out for us in His Word. We can begin to live as a people with a greater mission than just making ourselves comfortable on earth, a more significant challenge than just getting to work by 9am every day, and a more extraordinary passion than making it to a Friday night after a busy week. We hope far more than anything this world can offer us. A hope that lies in the promise of a life to come when this one ends.

However, with that hope comes a challenge, mission, and passion that we need to put into action. Many people in our own countries do not know Jesus. There is a lost world, many of whom do not know anything about this future hope we have been privy to.

Therefore, we have been left with a mission by God to go out and make it known to people.Mission is not only going overseas to tell people who don't know about Jesus, we need to get out our front door.

So on our final day, I want to leave you with a challenge. There are people in your world who need to know about a Saviour who loves them, who died for them, who wants to walk with them and help them. They need to know about the hope of Heaven and the reality of Hell. You can reach them, teach them, love them and lead them into the Kingdom. God has you in their life for a reason.

We have a reason to hope, but let us not become complacent in our lives because we know the truth. Let us reach out to others and pull them off a pathway leading to Hell and bring them with us to our confident hope of Heaven. You know the truth, you have read this book- why not pass it along to someone you know needs to hear it? Dare to hope, reach, love, serve and teach- someone reached once out to you.

Dare to hope. We have a reason that will never end, never change and never fail- His name is Jesus.

Dare to hope

Thank you for purchasing and reading this book.
I hope it has blessed, challenged and encouraged you in your walk with Jesus.
Why not pass it on to someone else who would benefit from reading it, or start all over again and see what else Jesus wants to say to you through it.
A review on Amazon following reading this would be so greatly appreciated to help encourage more people to invest in their walk with God.

For more info visit
www.amy-lennox.com

Printed in Great Britain
by Amazon

85270767R00108